CRUMBS

Ann Conway

Proverbs 3:5-6

CRUMBS

Will I Trust?

The Memoir Of
ANN CONWAY

ISBN 979-8887570-72-3

 TheAnnConway@gmail.com

 @theannconway

<u>DEDICATION</u>

To my son, Kevin,

who challenges me . . . stretches me . . .
and inspires my life.
You are an incredible son and a remarkable man.
I am privileged that you call me Mom.

TABLE OF CONTENTS

ACKNOWLEDGMENTS

Writing a memoir about ones own life is a surreal process and I could not have accomplished it without the encouragement and support of incredible friends.

I am forever grateful to my dear friend Bev Swanson who relentlessly encouraged me for years to write my story. She took my early long ramblings and scribblings, devoting extraordinary hours and days and turning them into a readable book.

I want to thank my friend Donna Rees for her amazing editorial expertise and being my consistent and enthusiastic cheerleader throughout this project. I am so grateful God brought us together in His perfect timing.

To our remarkable friends and family who walked along side us throughout our journey. Although I would have liked to, it was impossible to mention each of you individually. You have no idea how you impacted our lives and how God used you to affirm His faithfulness and trustworthiness over and over.

I thank God for you and your loving and prayerful support that will always be a part of my story and my memories. It is a result of your efforts and support that helped bring this memoir to life.

FOREWORD

YOU ARE ABOUT TO TAKE A JOURNEY with Ann Conway as she encounters happiness and clarity, pain and hurt, confusion and unanswered questions.

During the course of each person's life, there will be a blend of both good times and difficult times, happy events and sad encounters, healthy seasons and unhealthy setbacks. No two life stories are the same. The situations and experiences that seem fair to some seem unfair to others, but we will not be emotionally free to move forward if we're bound by memories of past hurts and painful encounters. You can't drive a car forward looking in a rearview mirror.

Sometimes it's an easy choice to go forward when we understand meaning and motives. At other times we have little choice but to accept life when we don't have details and things don't make sense.

Life gives us a choice to trust ourselves and those we are surrounded by or to distrust ourselves and those with whom we have challenging relationships. It's not a matter of "Do I move on?" or "Can I move on?" but rather a choice of "Will I move on?"

When life events don't give answers, can I trust God and move forward? Not can I trust, but will I trust?

Ann's story is descriptive of her life journey rather

than prescriptive as she describes the circumstances she experienced. It is not intended to be a formula for others. It is a description of choices she made in the crucible of challenges and faith. She faces her fears with faith and has answered the question of "Will I trust?"

As you read Ann's story, I hope you will be encouraged to face your unanswered questions and fears to move forward with faith and a renewed sense of trust and purpose in life.

Dr. Ron L. Braund
President of Family Business Transitions, Marriage and
Family Therapist and Author

Chapter 1

CRACKER CRUMBS

AN AVALANCHE OF TEARS THREATENED to fall as I turned around for one last look at my family and friends and then nervously stepped into the huge Boeing 707. I found Seat 12-A; no one was seated anywhere near me.

As I anxiously buckled my seat belt, my excitement turned to panic. *What was I doing?* It was my first time on an airplane—a 23-hour flight halfway around the world alone. The events surrounding the wedding, honeymoon, and preparation to join my new husband in Japan had given me little time to think about the actual trip. My inexperience as a traveler was only part of my youthful naïveté. My focus had been on becoming Mrs. Sam Conway and joining my handsome military husband in Japan. We had been married for only three weeks and it had all been so romantic.

As the plane ascended, I watched the only world I knew grow smaller and smaller. I felt a wave of trepidation that I had never felt before. I focused on the reason I was here: I was going to be with Sam!

I knew Sam was the man of my dreams the first time I saw him. I had prayed God would bring us together, and now I was his wife. Sam loved me and he loved the Lord, and I was going to be the best wife ever! I couldn't wait to be back in his arms, yet I felt fear pulling at my resolve. *Who gets married and flies halfway around the world to live in a foreign land for two years? I won't know anyone there except Sam, and I don't speak Japanese!*

A year ago I didn't even know Sam. We dated for three months and got engaged, and then two weeks later he received orders to report for duty in Japan. For eight long months, through hundreds of letters, we got to know each other. He flew home for our wedding and a brief honeymoon and then had to return to Japan, where I was now joining him. I sighed and looked out of the airplane window as I left all I had ever known.

The fact that we hadn't spent much time together loomed large. *What if we didn't get along when we were together every day? What if I didn't like Japan?* Sam made almost no money as a soldier, but he had made our move sound like a fabulous adventure. *What if it wasn't?* I was beginning to feel more apprehensive and very alone.

As soon as the "seat belt sign" was turned off, I stood to retrieve a pillow from the overhead bin and discovered there were only a handful of passengers on my 23-hour overseas flight. Not only did I have a complete row to myself, but I couldn't even see another passenger without standing. A stewardess came to my seat, offering breakfast. The beautiful silver tray was like a still-life painting of eggs Benedict, croissants, and fresh fruit. It looked delicious, but I wasn't very hungry, and I could only imagine how expensive a meal like that on a beautiful silver platter must be. I politely declined and thought about how proud Sam would be of my self-control. I leaned back in the seat, feeling better.

Sam and I would be okay. I wanted to be a good wife and knew that conserving our meager funds was a good way to begin. One of my girlfriends had taken a train trip the previous year and reported how expensive the food was. I concluded that if food on a train was that expensive, it must cost much more on an international flight. Reclining my seat and closing my eyes, I replayed the past year in my mind.

The day Sam stepped inside the door of my church, it was as though was he wearing a suit of shining armor and riding a white horse! The church was located near Washington, D.C. and Andrews Air Force Base, so it was not unusual for military guys to visit our church. However, this one stood out to me as special. No guy that good-looking had darkened our church doors in a very long time!

As the church pianist, I had a huge advantage over the other single girls, since they were all facing the front. From the platform, I could scrutinize each and every "potentially single guy" as he entered the sanctuary. I positioned my chair beside the large fern intended to hide the pianist from the congregation so that I could see him. Our eyes met more than once, and I was sure he smiled at me. *I had to meet this guy and find out more about him!*

My plan was to bolt from the platform at the close of the service to welcome him, but that day the organist picked a three-page postlude, and it seemed like it would never end. By the time I was able to dart from the platform, he was nowhere to be found.

I could hardly wait for the next Sunday, when I took extra care with my choice of clothes, hairstyle, and makeup. My knight returned and sat in the same spot. This time I was sure he smiled specifically at me, but by the time I got down from the platform, once again he was gone.

The next Sunday the unbelievable happened: he walked into our life-group class. I needed to know who he was before he slipped away again, so while everyone else was distracted, I rushed over to him with a 3 x 5 card I found in my Bible and introduced myself as the class secretary. I smiled and explained how the class needed his name and address for our records. He obligingly filled out the card, which I promptly and smugly tucked into my Bible. I left church that day hugging my Bible with its precious contents. I now knew his name was Sam.

It later became obvious that knowing his name and address got me no closer to knowing him. I kept the card in my Bible, because that seemed like the spiritual thing to do, and every day I would hold the card and pray that God might give me the chance to know Sam. Valentine's Day was approaching, so I took the opportunity to make my move. I purchased what I believed to be a lovingly appropriate valentine and hesitantly mailed it to him. The front of the card said: "Every time I think of you, this happens ..." and on the inside a little heart sprang up and jiggled like crazy.

After I mailed it, I nervously wondered if it had been appropriate to do so. I had included a scripture verse, Proverbs 3:5–6, so he would know I was spiritual. To ensure he didn't think I was being too forward, I had signed it "guess who."

As the sunlight disturbed my fitful nap on the plane, I stretched and raised my seat to more of a sitting position. The stewardess approached with another tray of delightful food. It looked wonderful. I was almost tempted to take it, but I knew food that looked that good had to be very expensive. Again I remembered how appalled my friend had been at the cost of just a sandwich on her train, so I graciously declined the stewardess's offer.

Looking at my watch, I realized I still had a long flight ahead of me. I wondered what our life would be like there. *Would we ever be able to afford luxury food like that which was offered on this plane?* Sam wouldn't always be in the military. *Would we have children?* I looked out of the window and thought about the enormity of God's world. *Where would He take us in the future? Would His direction always be as clear as it had seemed these past few months?*

I closed my eyes and thought about how quickly we had gone from "guess who" to being engaged. I had known from the beginning that Sam was the man I wanted to spend my life with, and God had heard my prayers. Sam did guess who had sent the card, and within three months we were engaged and looking forward to getting to know each other better when his assignment for Japan came through.

Relaxing with the memories, I rested as Japan Airlines swept me around the world to my Sam. Every two hours, the stewardess brought incredible trays of wonderfully appealing food. As I gazed at the many choices she offered—beautiful cheesecakes, chocolates, and fruit, my resolve to keep our meager budget under control was waning. I was getting hungry, but my will to be a good wife was strong. I smiled, thanked her, and continued to refuse her offers.

Throughout the day, the stewardess, who now appeared more annoying than adorable, offered me everything from a hot sandwich plate to sushi to filet mignon with all the dressings. I looked at the supper tray without a smile and told her, "No, thank you," and requested another glass of water.

After passing on the supper tray, I remembered that in the bottom of my purse were a couple packets of saltines from a restaurant where I had eaten the week before. I dug around until I found them. While the others on the plane enjoyed their gourmet meals, I begrudgingly ate my crackers and drank my water. *I am hungry, but I will stick to my good intentions.*

Shaking the last of the crumbs into the palm of my hand and licking my finger to get every last one, I was determined to start my new life right. I would not spend money we couldn't afford to spend on luxury foods. *Anyway, by tomorrow I'll be in Japan with Sam!*

After 18 hours on that plane, my initial resolve was only a shadow of a memory. I reasoned that my new husband wouldn't want me to starve to death before I reached him, so I was going to buy the next tray of food no matter how much it cost. *Surely just one meal wouldn't be that expensive.*

When the next tray arrived, I reached for my purse as I smiled at the stewardess and asked how much the food she was offering cost. Imagine my surprise when I learned that the meal was included in the cost of the ticket! All that food made available to me yesterday—the food that I had repeatedly turned down—was already paid for! I had refused to partake of what was already mine.

So many times over the years I have thought about that flight. Everything, including filet mignon, eggs Benedict, and chocolate mousse, had been mine while I stubbornly ate crackers. How many times since then had I willfully walked around eating stale, dry crackers out of the bottom of my purse when God had supplied and *paid for* me to be eating filet mignon and eggs Benedict? The few well-meaning friends who had given me all kinds of flight advice had not told me that the incredible delicacies and great meals on my flight were paid for.

Unfortunately, I have found this scenario can be true in our Christian walk as well. We are quick to give our opinion and advice when it comes to the "rules" about being a Christian, but we fail to tell people about God's provision of an abundant life and the incredible, personal relationship we can have with Jesus Christ. Through the years, I would come to understand what Jesus meant in John 10:10 when He offered us an abundant life that was far more abundant than I originally had believed.

It was nearly midnight when I stepped off of the plane and finally put my arms around my new husband. After our two-week separation, he was just as happy to see me as I was to see him. We walked out of the Tokyo airport, and I quickly learned that the man I had married was a very resourceful guy.

Two days prior to my departure, I had received a telegram from the United States Government "strongly suggesting" that I not go to Japan. Due to the war in Vietnam and escalating tension in the area, they would not give us housing on the Air Force base and were not obligated to give me any base privileges. Rather than deterring Sam, that information had merely challenged him, a trait I would witness over and over throughout our life together.

Sam met me in a multicolored (due to varying shades of rust) car he had negotiated into the deal with the house furnishings he had purchased for us. I was surprised as he excitedly told me how I was going to love our new home. It had been only two weeks since we had returned from our honeymoon, so I realized he had worked a miracle. Sam had rented a tiny, two-bedroom home and purchased all of the furniture and the car for a total cost of $250! My new husband was amazing! I could hardly wait to see it.

As we drove through the Tokyo traffic on that dark night, Sam gave me the details I would need to know since he would be leaving for work at the base hospital in only a few hours. He explained that our new home was in a typical Japanese rice paddy neighborhood, and one of our neighbors spoke a little English. The house had two bedrooms, a living room, a kitchen, and a bathroom and was around 600 square feet, but since I didn't know how much or how little 600 square feet was, that detail meant nothing.

He also explained that most families in the neighborhood lived without hot water, but he had arranged for us to have our own hot water heater installed. He explained in great detail what the new unit would look like, how it worked, and how it was to be installed. A gas line would be run into the house, and there would be an open flame under a water tank in the bathroom.

He had to contract with several men: one to install a heating unit, one to hook up the gas line, and a third to deliver and set up the tall tank that would be squeezed into the corner of our bathroom.

By the time we reached our new home it was the middle of the night and my head was swimming with the facts and details. Sam opened the sliding doors onto the tatami-covered floors and swept me up into his arms to carry me over the threshold. My heels sank deep into the woven mats (tatamis) when he put me down. He laughed and grabbed the slippers by the door, telling me I'd get used to taking off my shoes everywhere! Although it was rather dark with only one lamp in each room, our new home looked like a paradise to me.

As morning broke a few hours later, Sam explained that the first man coming would be the one with the heating unit for the corner of our bathroom. Sam left for the base at 7 a.m., and I was alone. In the sunlight, I got a look at what 600 square feet looked like when divided into five rooms. All the walls were like sliding doors, so when they were opened, it created the illusion of bigger space. After my long, 23-hour flight and a short night of sleep, I was just glad to be here with Sam in a place of our own. To my newlywed heart, it was like a little slice of Heaven.

Deciding the first thing to do was to unpack my bags I pulled my suitcase onto the bed. As I took items out and looked around the tiny room, I heard someone open the sliding door that led into my house. A bit panicked that I was no longer alone, I slowly slid back the wall that formed the bedroom and peered out into my living room. There stood a little old man with large, bucked teeth and a crumpled hat. Realizing this must be the first of the three men Sam had told me would come today, I was a little surprised that he had come so early and that he hadn't knocked before entering. I hesitantly slid the bedroom wall fully open and smiled at my first house-guest.

Seeing me, the little man bowed from the waist. Since I didn't know the Japanese word for *hello*, I merely bowed back. He didn't speak, but as I stood up he bowed again, so I did also. As I stood up, he bowed again, so I did also. We continued this bobbing up and down until I was almost dizzy. Not realizing that as a guest in my home, he was obligated to bow each time I did, I finally stopped him with my hand on his shoulder and said I was glad to meet him.

He smiled back at me and began to speak in Japanese.

Having no idea what he said, I pointed to the bathroom and told him the water heater would go in the corner. He nodded but didn't move.

"Water heater in corner," I repeated as I pointed to the bathroom. Again he smiled and bowed. Since I didn't know what else to do, I grabbed his sleeve and dragged him through the bedroom to my postage stamp-sized bathroom and pointed to the corner. "The water heater goes there," I told him.

The man nodded again, but this time he didn't smile. Wondering where Sam had found this guy and why he didn't go get his tools and start working. I told him to wait a minute, and I hurriedly left the bathroom to grab a pack of matches. When I returned, he was still standing by the tiny 3 x 3-foot bathtub, so I squeezed past him and knelt down on the floor. He just stared at me, so I grasped his sleeve again and pulled him down next to me. Now we are both kneeling in the corner of the tiny bathroom, pressed between the wall and the tub.

"Fire," I said as I pointed to the floor. Appearing concerned and confused, he looked from the corner back to me. Taking the match I had retrieved from the kitchen, I lit it and leaned forward holding the match near the floor.

The man smiled, nodded, and said, "Ah, so."

I wasn't sure why it took this much work for him to understand where the heating unit was to be placed, but I was glad we seemed to be making progress. I smiled until the funny little man with the hat on his head reached into his pocket, pulled out a cigarette, and leaned into the lit match I was holding in the corner of the bathroom. He lit his cigarette, sat back up, and puffed away, while we were both still kneeling in the corner of my bathroom.

The challenge of my new circumstances was becoming clear. Not knowing that it was then a custom in Japan for women to light men's cigarettes, I sat with my face barely a foot from the bucktoothed little old man and stared as he smoked his cigarette and smiled at me.

Exasperated, I stood and pulled him back to his feet by his sleeve. I dragged him through the house, out the front door, and across the street to the house Sam said had an English-speaking owner. As we approached the little square house that matched mine, the front door slid open and an older Japanese woman watched the young, American girl dragging the cigarette-smoking, old man across the street. "Do you speak English?" I asked her.

"English?" she responded and nodded. "A little."

"Will you tell this man that the water heater goes in the corner of the bathroom?"

The little old man and my new neighbor chattered back and forth for a minute.

Then she very seriously explained: "The man is very confused. He doesn't know what you are wanting from him. He is the laundry man. He stopped by to see if you have any clothes to wash."

That was my first introduction to life in Japan … and each day brought a new adventure.

Chapter 2

THE JOYS OF JAPAN

WE FELL IN LOVE WITH JAPAN and the Japanese people. We loved it so much that Sam put in a request to the Air Force for a one-year extension, which they gladly granted us. With the Vietnam War escalating, they were happy to give an extension to someone willing to add an extra year to his four-year commitment, especially one in the medical field overseas.

Over those three years, I realized how much Sam and I had grown up together and how it had solidified our relationship. We had no television, radio, phone, newspaper, or family there. We really only had each other. Our love grew as we learned to know one another better and as our knowledge of God grew. It was like an extended honeymoon as we worked and played and loved halfway around the world from the complications of social pressures and extended family.

Since we lived in a small community with the Japanese people, we totally embraced their way of life, and they seemed to appreciate it. I was able to obtain a job outside of Tokyo in an English-speaking Christian school as administrative assistant to the headmaster. Since I was the only English-speaking person on the administrative staff, the other gals in the office took great delight in teaching me conversational Japanese.

When Sam's tour of duty was over, we reluctantly left Japan. I'll never forget the flight back to the United States. We boarded a military aircraft full to capacity with soldiers all dressed in fatigues. Most were returning from Vietnam after a stopover at the base in Tokyo. To my surprise, I was the *only* female on the plane. I was crying, having said goodbye to my neighbors and friends whom I had grown to love. For the first time in my life, these were my and Sam's friends ... not friends of my parents or from the church I'd grown up in, but friends we had made as a couple. It was just "different"!

Most of the soldiers seemed to hardly move on that flight. Many slept. It was cramped and not at all like my flight to Japan. Many of them seemed to be annoyed by my tears. Most had been overseas and away from their loved ones and friends for a year or more, and naturally were thrilled to be on their way home. Several soldiers asked Sam what was wrong with me, and he would reply that I just hated to leave Japan. I overheard one guy mutter under his breath, "That woman is crazy."

Finally, a soldier came down the aisle handing each of us a small box of rations, which contained a tiny can of potted meat, a pouch of something indistinguishable, and some crackers. I had to smile ... the irony of it all: *crackers!* I had experienced an abundant life in Japan, not financially (sadly, often we think that is what it is all about), but in every other area of my life God had grown me, stretched me, and provided the most amazing and abundant three years, and I was grateful!

Although I knew God would take care of us, I wondered what our life would be like outside of the military. Sam had no idea what he wanted to do at this point in his life. Buckled in that seat on the airplane, I was reminded of the apprehensiveness I had felt on my flight over and how I had learned to trust God ... and *not* rely on my cracker crumbs!

It felt a little like I was beginning to crawl out of an incredible chrysalis into the unknown. While I wanted to see us soar like butterflies, I was wary of our future. Sam and I had shared everything together for three amazing years and had truly become each other's best friend, confidant, and partner in every area of our lives. *What would the next three years look like?*

We were headed to Tampa, Florida, to make it our new home. Although I was trusting God to continue to lead and guide us, I was unaware of how minuscule my trust actually was and had very little comprehension of what the "abundant life" may entail.

Chapter 3

BROKEN BONES, PAIN AND JOY

WE RELOCATED TO TAMPA, where Sam's parents and four younger siblings (two sisters who were married and two younger brothers) still resided and we were suddenly surrounded by family I had met only once before our wedding. Even though I had been Sam's wife for three years, his family and I really didn't know one another. From the moment we stepped into their home, I was determined to come across as the perfect wife and homemaker. I wanted the mother that Sam loved to be impressed with how well I could take care of her son.

Mrs. Conway was busy getting supper ready when we arrived. I offered to help her, but she assured me she had everything under control. She was making all of Sam's favorite dishes. We talked a little, and I again offered to help, but she insisted she didn't need any help.

I looked around the kitchen and decided that I could wash the dishes and pans in the sink as a way of making myself useful. I crossed the small kitchen and reached into the sink to grab a dirty cup. Unaware that Mrs. Conway had just drained boiling water from a pan of potatoes into the sink, as I turned the cup over to empty it, the boiling water scorched my hand.

With a muffled shriek, I dropped the cup and ran from the kitchen to the hall bathroom. Closing the door, I tried not to cry as I quickly threw open the medicine cabinet to search for something to put on my burning, throbbing hand—I certainly did not want to appear incompetent to my in-laws.

The medicine cabinet had the usual toothpaste, aspirin, and nail polish remover. There was also some ointment that I figured could only help. I grabbed it and squeezed gobs of it onto my throbbing hand. I continued to rub it in, and to my amazement it began to work. It seemed as though the burning was starting to ease.

The door opened and Mrs. Conway poked her head in, asking if I was okay. She said she had been worried when I bolted out of the kitchen as though being chased. Not wanting to confess my foolishness, I began to rub my hands together briskly.

"I was just putting a little of this ointment on my hands," I said as I smiled.

With eyes as big as saucers, she asked, "Do you always do that?"

"Oh, yes"—I replied. "I love to keep ointment on my hands."

"You always put Preparation H on your hands?" she asked incredulously. Since no one in my family had ever had hemorrhoids, I had no idea what Preparation H was.

"Sure!" I assured her, continuing to rub it into my hands. "Preparation H, I, J—you name it; I'll use it."

Mrs. Conway frowned and returned to the kitchen. I took a deep breath and put the top back on the long nozzle of the tube. My hands were now tingling, impressing me with how well this stuff worked.

By the time I got to the supper table, my hands were numb. Passing dishes and eating was challenging with numb hands, but I believed I managed to make a good first impression. When Mrs. Conway was adamant that Sam and I sit as guests and let her clean up, I easily acquiesced.

They could not have been too impressed with this odd girl their oldest son had married. For one thing, she seemed strange and clumsy. I was so concerned with their perception of me that I didn't let them see me at all. Instead of making a good impression, I came across as incompetent and peculiar.

Sam and I settled into our new life in Florida. It was quite an adjustment from the romantic isolation of Japan. Our life was flooded with Conways who were thrilled to have Sam back in their life. Not only was I readjusting to the States, but I also was living near family I didn't know very well. Sam, however, seemed happy to fall back into his old big brother and son roles, which sometimes left me feeling neglected.

It was a period of major adjustment as Sam was also trying to decide what to do with his life now that he was no longer in the military. By the end of the first year, we had set boundaries with family and settled into a happy, comfortable routine. As Sam continued to enjoy being near his family, I longed for a family of our own.

Using the expertise he had acquired in the United States Air Force, Sam opened a dental laboratory. We became involved in a local church, and together Sam and I asked the Lord to use us to fulfill His purposes for our lives. We were also praying for a baby. When month after month passed with no signs of pregnancy, we decided to seek medical assistance.

As a young boy, Sam had undergone a surgery that had the potential of leaving him sterile as an adult. The doctors told us pregnancy was improbable; however, it was not impossible. We tried to not give up hope, yet each month brought another wave of disappointment. It's hard to long for a baby and have arms that are empty year after year. We had been married for six years, and although we didn't lose faith in a God of miracles, we fought discouragement over the prospect of not having a family.

When my parents and grandfather visited us in Florida, we decided to take them to Disney World. On the second day of their visit, we departed from Tampa with Sam and my dad buckled into the front seat of our car. My mother, grandfather, and I snuggled into the back seat. At that time, seat belts for the back seats were not available. It was a beautiful, sunny day as we zipped along the highway.

We were halfway there when suddenly a flagman stepped onto the fast lane of the interstate waving a flag to stop traffic to allow a man on a riding lawn mower to cross the road. In an effort to avoid hitting the flagman, Sam swerved into the right lane—at the same time, a large fuel tanker truck also swerved and hit the right, rear quarter panel of our car, propelling us into the air.

Instantly the day changed from the delight of expectation to the horror of twisting metal and flying glass and the repeated impact of our car violently slamming against asphalt as it barreled down the embankment of the highway overpass to the road below.

In what seemed to be a surreal, slow-motion experience, our car rolled six times, catapulting my grandfather out the rear windshield. My mother was thrown only partially through the rear windshield, so with each roll of the car she was repeatedly thrust against the asphalt. My head went through the side window of our car, so with each flip I was viciously thrown back and forth, in and out, breaking bones as my shoulders were slammed over and over into the metal window supports.

Finally the car came to a stop, upside down. After the crash, there seemed to be moments of silence, extreme silence like a "piercing sound in your ear" silence. The crash was disorienting ... it was loud ... and then everything became still and quiet after the car came to a sudden stop, landing on its roof. I could see my mother's broken body hanging halfway out the rear windshield and blood was pouring profusely from an open area in the back of her skull. I was sure she was dead.

I went in and out of consciousness until the paramedics arrived to dislodge us from the gasoline-soaked car. My grandfather's back was fractured, and he was immediately taken to Tampa, where the best neurologists would be available.

As I was pulled out through the window, the paramedics became aware of my many broken bones and immediately wrapped my body as they feverishly attempted to stop the bleeding in my mother's head. The ambulances transported my mother and me to a local hospital as the EMTs were tweezing shards of glass from our faces.

Sam and my dad had been wearing seat belts, and they both were able to walk away with only bruises. After many X-rays and examinations, they determined that my mother had no broken bones; however, as a result of being repeatedly slammed against the asphalt, she had third-degree burns on her back and arms and needed hundreds of stitches. I was put into a type of "body cast" to immobilize my arms, as my sternum, both clavicles and shoulder blades, and most of my ribs were broken.

Over the next three days I was heavily medicated to prevent me from moving. They had folded my arms across my chest and bound my body, mummy-style. They also had sutured my mother's head and other injuries and bandaged her body and head, so that all I could see when I came out of medicated sleep was her mummified body, with slits where her eyes and mouth would be. Seeing her like that sent me into hysterics, and I would immediately be given another injection to take me back into oblivion.

As Sam and my dad were leaving the hospital on the third night after the accident, they encountered a man crying in the parking lot. He said he had just received devastating news about his wife's health and explained that although she had great faith, he didn't believe but wanted to.

Sam and my dad explained how and why Christ had sacrificed His life and how this man could have abundant life in Jesus. The man bowed his head and gave his life to Christ as his wife watched from the window of her hospital room. The next day, we were told she had been praying for her husband for 30 years. My dad told me the story, saying that made the accident worth it all! The men in my life were trusting God after such a horrific wreck even though those they loved the most were suffering. In my extreme physical pain, I wondered if I would ever have enough faith to say such a thing.

Today I can say that suffering is worth the lessons we learn from it, but it took a long time and many more unexpected turns in my life for me to be able to say those words. With time and testing, I learned to be thankful that our sovereign Lord had answered that dear lady's prayer of 30 years by having us at that exact location on that specific day. I cannot wait to meet both of them in Heaven.

On day four, a physician friend of ours drove to the small-town hospital where we were being treated to encourage Sam. He was appalled when he looked at my unrecognizably swollen face and realized that no one had removed my contact lenses. Concerned about the level of care we were being given, he gently unwound the strips of bandage that bound my arms to my body. The minute he saw my left arm, he walked Sam into the hallway and told him it was imperative that I be moved to Tampa immediately!

My left arm was the size of my thigh. He could tell I

was bleeding internally; the blood was accumulating in my arm and the bandages were preventing anyone from noticing or treating me. Our friend made the necessary arrangements for our transfer, and within a few hours my mother and I were on our way back to Tampa. The orthopedic surgeon explained to Sam that another day's delay could have caused the loss of use of my entire arm. It was also discovered that over one inch of bone in the midsection of each of my clavicles was missing from the repeated slamming against the car window supports. The doctors hoped that over time, the damaged areas would rejoin naturally, thus avoiding the necessity of surgically implanting pins.

Although the three of us were healing, we continued to experience tremendous pain. As soon as my mother and grandfather were able to travel, they returned to their North Carolina homes. I remained confined to a recliner 24 hours a day, giving me a lot of time to think and reflect.

I had so many questions for God about the abundant life He promised. Going to Disney World had been my idea. *What if I hadn't insisted we go? Was this all my fault? What if we had taken a different route that morning?* With so much time on my hands, playing the blame game was easy. All of the if-only questions plagued me every day: *Is God really sovereign? How does He figure into things like this? Couldn't He have prevented all of it? Is God really faithful?* These were the issues I wrestled with as I sat in that recliner day after day. I slowly began to feel peaceful as I found answers, yet God still had so much more to show me and teach me!

It was three months before all of the casts and support-wraps were totally removed, and new X-rays revealed that while my ribs and shattered shoulder blades were healing, there was no new calcification of bone in the clavicles. The orthopedic surgeon said the best thing for me to do would be to get pregnant, which would likely build up the calcium in my body. He flippantly chuckled and told us to "get busy" or we would be looking at multiple surgeries to rejoin the clavicle bones on both sides.

There could have been no less comforting words told to a couple struggling with infertility. My body was not doing *anything* normally: my sleep was almost nonexistent, my cycles were totally off-kilter, and it was painful to move, much less be touched. Yet this doctor's remedy was to get busy! I was concerned about how that was going to work, but I had promised to trust God and that was just what I was going to do.

I continued to see the orthopedic surgeon. The next month, on my follow-up visit, he decided not to do any X-rays just in case I was pregnant. He had more faith than I did, but we continued to pray. Then, one morning soon after that, I became overwhelmed with the smell of bacon cooking and ran to the bathroom to throw up. Over the next few days, smells continued to nauseate me and I worried that I'd developed an ulcer in response to the stress in my life.

It wasn't long before it became apparent that what I had not dared to even hope was true: I was actually pregnant. God had made something good out of all the trauma and pain. He had my attention in a new way. I truly wanted to put my life unconditionally into His hands. As my broken body was healing, God was giving us the child for whom we had prayed. I realized only God had known when I would need this pregnancy for healing. He is always in the details!

Chapter 4

FRESH BERRIES AND MERINGUE

I WAS BEGINNING TO UNDERSTAND HIS WAYS, feeling more confident in giving Him control. During the months of my pregnancy, there were no X-rays, so we just trusted God for the growth and healing of my clavicles. Our precious Christen finally arrived, and she was the delight of our life. We were thankful that she weighed only 6 pounds at birth, because through therapy I had built my strength up to lift only 5-pound weights. As Christen grew, the strength in my arms and shoulders slowly returned. She became the best physical therapy God could have provided.

Soon after Christen's birth, X-rays revealed small calcium deposits on each side of the broken bones. Over time they grew together and provided me with what appears to be rough mountain ridges where the smooth bones once were. God had healed my clavicles.

I was so happy to be living in my perfect little world. We had a new home, a beautiful baby, friends, and a growing business. One day when Christen was 2 years old, Sam came in and said that for over a year he had been wrestling with the Lord over a decision. He felt that God was calling him to go back to school for a degree in

Biblical Studies. I was shocked! However, we had made a commitment early in our marriage that if and when God would lead us, we would follow. We also had agreed to pray about decisions, and if either of us didn't have peace, we would wait.

It didn't take long for God to make His plan clear to me as well. After a couple of months of looking into colleges around the country and putting our house up for sale, God's plan for us became very clear, and we soon made our way to Lynchburg, Virginia. Lynchburg was a unique city in that it had 48 dentists—and not one dental laboratory. As he had hoped, Sam was able to get into the Biblical Studies program, and he also opened a dental laboratory.

Sam's personality was energized by change, so the move was easy for him. He quickly met and connected with new people. It was harder for me to adapt to new surroundings, so in my determination to make friends, I attended a women's luncheon held in a gorgeous 500-seat hotel banquet hall filled with beautifully decorated round tables. Upon entering, I quickly found a vacant seat and introduced myself to the table of well-dressed women. I attempted to casually join in the conversation about people and places I didn't know as we ate a rather mediocre meal.

Our lunch plates were cleared, and in what appeared to be the highlight of the event, we were served an incredible dessert consisting of a meringue nest filled with fresh berries of every kind; a thick, red sauce flowed over the berries and covered the sides of the meringue. It almost looked too good to eat.

My first attempt to pierce the Styrofoam-like meringue with my fork brought no results, so I discreetly pushed a little harder. Nothing. The women at my table were still talking, so when no one seemed to be looking, I laid my fork on the hardened meringue and with the base of my hand firmly punched the fork to break through the white confection. I watched in horror as the entire dessert was catapulted across the table, its target being the expensive, white wool suit of the woman who sat across from me.

What should have been merely an embarrassing situation became a nightmare as the woman felt the hit, looked down at the bright red spot on her chest, and shrieked, "I've been shot!" I quickly informed her she had not been shot, but my words were drowned by nearly 500 panicked women who were screaming, diving under tables, and running toward the exits.

I continued to assure everyone that the woman had not been shot, but no one listened. In record response time, I heard sirens and then realized that official-looking people were attempting to clear the room. The police were coaxing frightened women out from under the white cloth-covered tables. When they finally drew the woman in the white suit out and asked why she thought she had been shot, she replied, "I've seen people on TV shows who didn't know they were shot until they saw the blood." The long-planned, perfectly orchestrated luncheon was over before the singer and speaker had even been introduced. I left my first Lynchburg luncheon without making any friends.

Sam's studies were challenging, and the business was growing. I finally had made incredible new friendships, and then we received the most wonderful news: we were pregnant again! God blessed us with a son, Kevin. Four-year-old Christen was thrilled by the arrival of her baby brother.

Life was moving along as we perceived it should. We had trusted God and followed Him where we believed He wanted us to be. We were reaping all the blessings of the seeds of faith we had sowed. We were doing our part and believed God was doing His. We had prayed and obeyed and God was giving us an abundant life. I felt I had endured enough trauma in my life to prove to God that I trusted Him. He allowed me to be a loving wife to Sam and a devoted mother to my two babies and also to be involved in numerous ministries at our church. I was content yet, had no idea what was ahead for our little family.

Chapter 5

GOD WAS ALWAYS WAITING

ONE DAY WHEN KEVIN WAS 11 MONTHS OLD, Christen and I laughed as he toddled on chubby legs with a loaded diaper hanging to his knees. I scooped him up and put him on the changing table. As I removed his diaper, I was shocked to discover bright red blood and dozens of blood clots. With 4-year-old Christen in tow, we rushed to the pediatrician's office.

That was the beginning of a two-year journey as we went from hospital to hospital all across the country seeing 17 different specialists to try to stop the bleeding. I know what it is like to hold a sick baby through night after night. I've experienced long and sleepless nights in a hospital recliner, begging God to reveal to someone what was wrong with my child.

Some days Kevin would have a dozen bloody diapers, some days none. Fortunately, in the midst of all of this were normal days. Kevin was an active toddler interested in anything with wheels, following his father's love of racing at an early age. He constantly demanded to wear a helmet even to ride his little tricycle, because in his young mind he was always a race car driver.

Even through the good days, Kevin's illness was still

on my mind. Sam and I had trusted God through our years of infertility, but this somehow felt different to me. I trusted God to heal Kevin or at least give us a diagnosis, but my mother's heart still trembled with fear, worry, and a need to control. I struggled to trust God completely with whatever He wanted to do with my sweet little boy. Surely a God Who loved me would not take my child!

During many dark, sleepless nights in hospital rooms, I would cry out to God to heal my baby, to give us peace and patience with the many doctors who sent my little guy into uncontrollable screaming fits while providing us with no answers. Getting crackers from a hospital vending machine, I was often reminded of pulling crackers from my purse on that long-ago plane ride when amazing provisions were already paid for. "Please God," I would pray, "help me to trust You!"

God was always waiting when I turned to Him. He would give me the peace and love I really needed during those late-night, heartfelt prayers, but too often, with the light of day, I would begin to worry and fear again. Repeatedly I gave my baby son to God, only to try to take back control when the next bloody diaper appeared. *How could God ask me to surrender my son?*

After two long years, we heard about an alternative doctor and took Kevin to see him and told of all the specialists we had seen and the different antibiotics they had tried. Within a few minutes, the doctor calmly said: "I think your son is reacting to the antibiotics. When did this all start?"

I thought back and remembered Kevin had been given antibiotics for an ear infection shortly before the first bloody diaper appeared and had continued to be given a great variety of antibiotics throughout his treatments. This doctor took Kevin off all antibiotics and put him on an all-natural program of vitamins and supplements to replenish his system.

We had experienced 24 months of sleepless nights in and out of hospitals, fluctuating between prayer and panic and spending thousands of dollars, Within two weeks of stopping the use of antibiotics, there were no more bloody diapers, and Kevin began to get stronger and healthier.

God had led me through so many trials, starting with my life in a foreign country with no family or friends to the anguish of infertility to months of pain from an unforeseen accident and now these years with Kevin. With each lesson, God would remind me of eating those crackers in the bottom of my purse. I wanted so much to trust Him, yet many times I would continue to pick up those crumbs of worry and fear instead of feasting on the abundant life of peace, joy, and love that Jesus promised.

Chapter 6

CHRISTEN'S BLACK AND WHITE WORLD

PRECOCIOUS, INTUITIVE, AND CHALLENGING were words typically used to describe our cherub-faced, 7-year-old daughter. From the time she could talk and understand right from wrong, Christen's world was black and white. There were no grays for her, especially when it came to Christian living. Unfortunately, during Christen's early years, we were involved in a very legalistic church, which taught that in order to live a victorious Christian life, one must obey a lot of rules that identified which behaviors were acceptable and which ones were not.

Christen firmly believed that the many rules and restrictions we applied to our faith should apply to everyone. If someone taught her that Jesus said, "Judge not, lest you be judged," then she better not hear that person criticizing someone he or she had a problem with, because if she did, Christen would boldly remind that person of the Bible verse he or she had taught her. If God said it, that settled it for Christen. She would not stand for hypocritical behavior in us or anyone else who taught her. For her, hypocrisy was the ultimate sin.

Another of Christen's strong character qualities was

her passion, which was manifested in every part of her life. Whatever she did, she did to the extreme. The people she loved, she loved wholeheartedly. She was as loyal and enthusiastic as a golden retriever puppy.

Christen was a fun and happy child. She was stubborn, yet sensitive. She wanted to please—as long as what we were saying made sense to her. The dichotomy between wanting to please and needing to be right could swing her from joy to despair in the blink of an eye. Christen never had mere Christian examples in her young life—she had *heroes.* Her teachers, pastors, parents, all those she looked up to and loved had better not fall off that tall pedestal upon which she placed them.

Even as a child, Christen demanded the best from everyone she loved. She had lofty, honorable, and impossible expectations for those whom she trusted. She believed in them with all her heart, and therefore, when imperfections surfaced—as they inevitably would—she was not disappointed ... she was devastated. Her heroes never merely stumbled; they would free-fall from their heavenly positions, and Christen personally would absorb the impact. Sometimes she vocalized her feelings; sometimes she didn't. Either way, the hurt was tucked away in a heart that wanted to love the world. She was a happy child with grown-up eyes that didn't miss a thing.

Christen's gusto for life and her manner of not backing down when she knew she was right became a source of conflict for her, especially in school. She wouldn't hesitate to let her teacher know when she thought something was only a half-truth or had been inaccurately quoted. She would usually finish her lessons before her classmates did, and her impatience made it difficult for her to wait for the others.

The private Christian school she attended went through several scandals. Regretfully, the incidents involved her teacher and the children's pastor. As another of Christen's role models would fall, whether she spoke of it or not, she internalized each transgression as though it had been a personal assault against her.

By the middle of third grade, Christen's supper prayer would include pleas for God to convince Mommy and Daddy to homeschool her and her brother, Kevin. She was smart for her age, as well as bored with school and beginning to hate it.

Sam and I prayed about it, did a lot of research, and sought Godly counsel for quite a while before we decided to homeschool both Christen and Kevin. In doing so, we realized it would allow us to accelerate their education while providing them with unique life experiences and the ability to pursue their individual interests. We enrolled in an advanced educational program with weekly accountability, and both Christen and Kevin excelled in their studies and extracurricular activities with their peer groups.

Chapter 7

COW PATTIES, A FISHING BOAT AND ALBERTA

SAM AND I HAD STARTED WATCHING the TV program *This Old House,* in which the host would feature an old fixer-upper or abandoned house. Then, in the remarkable fantasy world of TV, in 30 minutes you were looking at an updated, beautiful, modern home that amazingly still maintained all of the grace, elegance, and charm of its original time period. The more we watched that show, the more intrigued we became with the concept of finding a property that we could fix up ourselves.

We began to talk about looking for land with an old, antebellum-style farmhouse on it. Sam began researching the fescue hay industry, and after a couple of trips North to visit the Amish to learn how to properly farm fescue, we set our sights on finding one of those 30-minute fixer-uppers and capturing the fescue hay market in Virginia.

I'll never forget the night when we were talking with friends and Sam began telling them of our plans and goals for a house and hay farm project. Our friend said he knew of an abandoned farm with a beautiful home that had been built in 1821, and it totally fit the criteria Sam had laid out. Despite the fact that it was 9 p.m., cold, and we were in the middle of a terrible storm, Sam and our friend drove to the farm in dark, blinding rain.

When they arrived they found the gate to the driveway locked, so they proceeded to climb the gate, which was easier than climbing the four-row-high barbed wire fence that surrounded the property. They ran down the quarter-mile-long driveway to get a closer look at the house.

When they returned, soaked to the bone and freezing, it was hard to tell if they were shaking due to the cold or the excitement as they both tried to describe this beautiful, huge, antebellum-style farmhouse. It was hard not to catch their enthusiasm.

For Sam, dawn couldn't come fast enough! He was up early and made breakfast for Christen, Kevin, and me. He excitedly announced that as soon as we ate, we were driving to the farm to see his amazing find. The drive took us to the absolute farthest point in Virginia, almost 30 miles from our current home. We were heading down the highway to Appomattox, where the Civil War had ended.

When I questioned the location, Sam assured us it wasn't as far as it seemed—we just weren't familiar with the country roads. As I was desperately trying to make note of the many turns en route to our destination, I wondered if Sam and I might be entering a personal civil war of our own.

We finally arrived at the gate, which had a chain and heavy padlock on it. This was just the first thing he had forgotten to mention. There were more unseen surprises to come after Sam's preview in a dark, blinding rain-storm. After we all managed to climb over the gate, or to put it more accurately, after I finally figured out how to get over the gate, we walked the quarter-mile down the driveway, dodging the cow patties, which became more numerous as we walked the long, winding drive. Eventually we got a glimpse of a huge farmhouse that did look big and stately. Beautiful columns rose in splendor across the front, and enormous black walnut trees surrounded the entire house. There was a wooden swing hanging between two trees, facing a large pond off to one side. We could see a guest house on the other side, with barns and outbuildings in the distance. It could have been a scene out of *Gone with the Wind!*

By now, the kids were running toward the house, squealing with delight. As Sam and I got closer, he admitted they had not gone into the house the night before due to the weather conditions and lack of light. Although we had been dodging those cow patties, we had not seen any cows and soon discovered why: there was no front door on this abandoned house, and the cows had taken it over as their shelter; Sam had to shoo them out before we could go inside. Even knowing about the cows, I was still surprised to find a 20-foot fishing boat sitting in the foyer. I cautioned the children to dodge the myriad of indoor cow patties.

The interior walls had been stripped down to the out-side walls, and it was obvious someone had entertained the idea of restoring the house and had given up. That should have been our first red flag. Actually, the cows and the boat were major red flags for me. As the kids excitedly ran throughout all three floors of the house making discovery after discovery, I was in a state of shock that Sam would even consider such a project!

Sam walked through this enormous house, pointing out the beautiful sets of French doors, still intact with their original glass, and the many windows with their original wavy glass. Beautiful fireplaces and original black walnut hardwood floors graced the entire house. Somehow as we talked about the architecture that dated back a century, the cow poop seemed to fade in importance. We began to talk and dream about what it could look like. I don't remember at what point the rose-colored glasses fell across our eyes.

We got to a place where it no longer mattered that the picturesque front porch was barely hanging on and huge portions of those beautiful columns had rotted away. I'm sure the entire house should have been condemned, and surely the porch wasn't safe, but as we stood there and looked out across the beautiful pond and rolling hills of hay, something happened. We declared right then and there that this would be our home, a beautiful sanctuary wherein to raise our children.

Much of that day is a blur, except that Sam found a huge, antique tractor in one of the outbuildings, and Christen discovered an original copy of *Black Beauty* in the loft of one of the barns. At that point, maybe we thought we'd find enough treasures on the property to help pay for it. Unfortunately, other than some antique glassware, there were no other significant discoveries.

We purchased the home and 60 acres of farmland for a good price and immediately hired a restoration construction crew to remodel the house. We quickly put our own home on the market, received a contract right away, and aligned our closing date with the promised completion of the farmhouse.

When the day for the closing of our home arrived, the farmhouse was nowhere near completion. There had been unforeseen problems at every turn. Enormous cost overruns happened during the first week and continued every week thereafter. As the date to move got closer, we tried to make adjustments almost every day in order to get an occupancy permit. To save on costs, we committed to painting the entire inside ourselves and decided to replace the beautiful front porch and columns later.

To honor the terms of the contract on our house sale, we packed up and put almost everything into storage before moving into a small, two-bedroom apartment to impatiently await the completion of our dream home. We convinced ourselves it wouldn't be hard to scale down for a couple months, since we were spending most of our free time at the farm anyway, trying to help move things along. Every day the kids and I were working on schoolwork, going to the farm, shopping for antiques, and going in and out of the apartment. One day as we were leaving, Christen pointed to an elderly woman standing outside and said, "There she is—that lady who is always watching us!"

"It's kind of creepy," Kevin joined in.

"Maybe she just wants to meet us," I advised them.

"Tomorrow we'll introduce ourselves to her when we leave."

I had previously noticed the elderly woman who lived in the apartment below us. She was hard not to notice. Each time I closed our apartment door and started toward the parking lot, she would step outside her door and watch me leave. The following morning, before we walked toward the car I stopped as she walked out of her door.

"Good morning," I said as I smiled. "My name is Ann, and these are my children, Christen and Kevin."

She introduced herself as Alberta. She said she was a widow and lived in the lower-level apartment alone. I told her I was happy to meet her, but we were in a hurry. I was hoping that the introduction would curb her curiosity about us.

Now that Alberta knew our names, however, she became bolder and began asking us where we were going when we left. I would often come and go many times during the day between shopping and school and working for Sam. Each time, she would corner me with questions about where I was going or what I was going to do that day. Sometimes she would even ask to ride along.

Starting out as an annoyance, Alberta became a daily aggravation. The children and I would try to hurry to the car to avoid her persistent questions. This tiny apartment life was getting to all of us as we entered our second month of it.

One night after supper, as Sam was leading us in family devotions, the three of us began to tell him about Alberta. The tiny apartment was taking on the feeling of a prison under the watchful eye of our door monitor.

"We think she listens for us to leave so she can get us on our way out," Kevin told his father.

"She's driving us crazy," Christen added.

Sam turned in his Bible to James 1:27 and read, "This is pure and undefiled religion in the sight of our God and Father, to visit orphans and widows in their distress." We talked about what that meant, and Sam explained that God wanted us to always be willing to reach out to those who could in no way give anything in return. He challenged us to reach out to Alberta since it was obvious she had nothing and maybe no one in her life.

When devotions were over, Christen wanted to take a piece of cake down to Alberta, which she did.

Christen ran back into the apartment, excitedly reporting that Alberta was so happy to receive the gift that she had shed tears of joy. Over the next few months that we lived there, Alberta became a part of our life. Every morning, either Christen or Kevin would run down with an egg sandwich for her. Every night, one of them would take her a plate of food for her supper. On Sundays she would go to church with us and stay for Sunday lunch.

Alberta didn't share much about her life, but she loved to listen to stories about ours. I started taking her to the store with me, where she would usually wait in the car. Often, she rode along when I went by the farmhouse to check on its progress. She smiled a lot, happy to just to be out of her apartment, and as much as possible, we began to include her in everything we did.

Finally the farmhouse was getting closer to completion. Sam, Christen, Kevin, and I began camping out at the farm on weekends. Christen and Kevin loved it, and Sam and I could get so much accomplished. The children thought of our times there as mini camping vacations. We even bought an old camper that was little more than sufficient for our weekend stays. We would be exhausted by Sunday night, but every hour we worked on the house made us an hour closer to one day moving in. Our nights in the camper officially ended the night we woke to find that a raccoon had joined us inside and was eating our food.

One Monday morning, I dropped Christen and Kevin off at a friend's house and was heading alone to the farm to spend the day working there. As I drove down the highway, I felt a prompting from the Lord to go back and check on Alberta. I reminded the Lord that I had a thousand things on my to-do list that day and that I'd have one of the children check on her when I returned home. I continued to drive, but the nagging feeling about Alberta would not let up. I wheeled my car around and drove back to the apartment, realizing that she had not stepped out to see us leave that morning.

As I walked to Alberta's door, I felt a knot in my stomach and loudly knocked. After repeated knocking and calling her name with no response, I opened the unlocked door. There, slumped over at the kitchen table, was the body of Alberta. I walked in to be sure of what was so obvious. We had often talked about her love and trust in the Lord, and now she was with Him.

I looked at her and thanked God that He had sent me back to check on her. *What if I had sent one of the children to check on her?* I didn't know why Alberta had been a part of our life in the apartment, but I was glad she had.

I ran up the steps and called 911. Within moments, a fire truck, ambulance, and four police cars had arrived. Suddenly, four police officers were surrounding me, firing questions: "WHY did I open the door? WHY did I go inside?" I was under intense interrogation and began to tremble and cry. *What could they be suspecting of me?* Now they wouldn't let me leave the apartment, which was starting to feel smaller and smaller.

They continued to fire questions at me as I cried, looking back and forth from them to dead Alberta. I begged to call my husband, and one officer finally agreed. He walked with me to my apartment, where I called Sam. Sam told me not to say anything else and that he would be right there. We walked back to Alberta's apartment, and within a few minutes Sam stormed in.

"This is OVER!" was all he said. He then took my arm and led me back up to our tiny apartment. I watched from the window as they put Alberta's body into the back of a hearse and drove off. Again, I thought about how God had placed this strange, eccentric old lady in our lives. When I picked the children up, I simply told them Alberta was in Heaven. We all cried together.

Four nights later, someone knocked on our apartment door. When I opened it, a distraught woman said she was looking for Christen and Kevin who lived upstairs.

She said she was Alberta's daughter from up North. We introduced ourselves, and she asked if we would walk back down to her mother's apartment with her.

Through tears, the daughter told us she had not seen her mother in many years, and while she was packing Alberta's things, she had found her mother's diary. Christen and Kevin were mentioned over and over. They had been the delight of her life these past few months. Because they had shown her mother so much love, the daughter believed anything Alberta had should go to them.

Alberta did not have much, but it turned out she was an avid reader. There were boxes and boxes of incredible books, many of which had never been unpacked. There were sets of updated encyclopedias and biographies and history, science, art, travel, music, and reference books. Most of them were expensive; some were collectible books, and all were in perfect condition. Christen and Kevin had just inherited a complete and beautiful library.

Along with the books, Alberta had boxes of unique items from foreign countries. We took them back to our apartment and wondered about the strange woman who had so many fun and exciting things from around the world. *Who had she been? What was she like when she was young? Why had she traveled so?* She had a daughter she had never spoken of, and yet she never had seemed angry or bitter.

At 90 years old, Alberta had been lonely and grateful for the smallest things. Christen and I laughed as we burrowed through a large box of Alberta's costume jewelry as though it were a grand treasure chest. God brought us to Alberta that she might enjoy Christen and Kevin in her final months on earth. He brought her to us to teach us what pure and undefiled religion really was. In the process, He blessed us with an amazing library that God had great plans for us to use in our homeschool adventure.

Chapter 8

LIVING IN "THIS OLD HOUSE"

LIVING THE "FARM LIFE" wasn't quite what we expected. We were more like a scene out of the old TV show *Green Acres*. I had heard it said, "You can't take the farm out of a gal!" I discovered you can't take the city out either! It was a 20-minute drive from the town of Lynchburg to any stores, and our closest neighbor was a mile away.

We were very secluded, so secluded that I was afraid on the nights when Sam was out of town. I put "Beware of the Dog" signs on the fence posts at the road every time he was away. One day when Sam stopped at the local Farm Supply Market, they asked him how his trip had been. They said they knew he had been gone, because I'd put up all of the signs! From that day on, we just left the signs up.

The acres of farmland were terraced for raising fescue hay, and we looked forward to the added income we would derive from the new business. However, our new venture as hay farmers did not go as well as expected. With the cost of hiring a local farmer to cut, bale, haul off, and sell it, we rarely broke even. We saved enough hay for our own animals and to fill the barns with hay for the kids to build hay-slides and forts.

Our kids enjoyed the farm life and were excited to acquire farm animals. Our first acquisitions were two kittens, which we had hoped would deter the mice from occupying the barns and outbuildings. While it took the cats a while to become good mousers, they wasted no time in becoming prolific kitten-creators, and before long we had no more mice—but dozens of cats on our farm!

We purchased two ponies, and much to our surprise (as well as to the man who sold them to us), one was pregnant! When the vet came to examine her, he informed us that she should not consume any fescue hay at all. This required us to build her a special pen, which meant we had to haul her food and gallons of water every day. Just like our beautiful antebellum farmhouse, the unforeseen expenses of owning and maintaining ponies and other animals truly blindsided us. We worked hard to put in a large garden, which the deer and bunny rabbits totally cleaned out and enjoyed. One positive feature of the farm, however, was that the pond, which had not been fished in for years, was so overstocked with fish that they would bite a hook immediately—with or without bait. This provided Kevin and his friends with hours of fishing enjoyment!

Sam had always loved racing anything with a motor, and with the fescue hay market now off of our agenda, Sam purchased dirt bikes for himself and Christen and Kevin to ride through the terraced fields. They spent hours riding, exploring, and soaring over those hills on their dirt bikes. It wasn't long before they progressed to racing go-karts, and Sam created a full-sized go-kart track with actual banked turns.

On Fridays, Sam always made sure his little char-treuse-green Datsun truck was full of gasoline, because Christen and Kevin would drive that stick-shift truck all over the farmland for hours on end, with the only stipulation being that Sam would have enough gas in the tank to get back to town on Monday morning. Kevin was only 6 years old and could barely see over the steering wheel. He would have to slide to the bottom of the seat in order to push the clutch to change gears. It was hilarious to watch, because when he did that, there was no driver visible in the truck! Many times they would burn a tank of gas every weekend, which was a lot of driving since they never left the farm.

I can remember standing at my kitchen window watching the kids fly by either on the dirt bikes or in that little green truck, making laps around the house and farm. Sometimes they'd have friends over and we'd load the back of the truck with hay and take them on long hayrides.

The farm was a haven for our family and a favorite place for our children's friends to visit. The kids had the dirt bikes, motocross bikes, Honda Odysseys, racing go-karts, paddle boats on the pond, and various small animals! We didn't have to invest in livestock, as our neighboring farm had horses and cows that ended up on our property more than on theirs. One animal that we didn't have, but I had always wanted, was a lamb ...

One evening, there was a knock at the front door. A neighboring farmer asked Sam to come and take a look at something he had in his trunk. Upon opening the trunk, Sam gazed at two little black lambs that were barely one day old. The farmer said that his ewe had delivered triplets and had rejected these two and he was wondering if Christen and Kevin would like to try to save them.

We took the tiny, weak lambs to our closest barn and laid them down on fresh hay. The farmer told us where we could purchase nursing bottles and specially formulated powdered milk for them if they survived the night.

Early the next morning, Sam and Kevin went to the local feed store and purchased the recommended items. The lambs nursed vigorously and required feeding every few hours. In time, they began to gain strength and soon were running, jumping, and playing. Christen would bathe, powder, and put diapers on her lamb and we allowed him to run around inside the house. The Biblical example of Jesus as our Shepherd and us as sheep became real, and we learned relevant lessons as we watched them grow.

The years we lived on the farm were unconventional, but we all loved it. Our life settled into a routine. Our homeschooling was going well, we were involved in our local church, and Christen and Kevin were both participating in youth programs and many extracurricular activities with peer groups.

Christen was taking horseback riding lessons and showing her standard poodles in dog shows. Kevin began competitive racing in the go-kart and Open Wheel Sprint Race car series.

Our dental lab business had grown exponentially,

and we now had numerous employees and satellite labs in neighboring towns. This growth enabled Sam to do what he loved: invest in the lives of others, and he began to search for individuals who were sincerely seeking to learn more about implementing God's ways in their lives. His search led him to the ministry of Motor Racing Outreach (MRO), a start-up ministry in Charlotte, North Carolina, that was devoted to reaching out to the racing community (specifically NASCAR), and to Christian Financial Concepts (CFC), a ministry started by Larry Burkett, located just outside of Atlanta, Georgia, that was devoted to teaching God's ways to handle finances, particularly to corporate leaders in the business world.

Sam began teaching weekly Bible studies for MRO to the team members in two NASCAR race shops—driving the four hours each way to Charlotte, North Carolina, every Tuesday to teach and mentor men who desired to learn more about God's ways. Once a month, he would teach a two-or three-day Business by the Book Seminar for corporate CEOs and business leaders all over the country (sponsored by CFC). God used him in the racing and corporate world in a significant way as he taught Godly principles of life by applying Biblical truths and sharing insights that he had gained personally through trial and error.

When CFC ministry headquarters received a request for the business seminar to be offered to leaders in the NASCAR community, Larry immediately called Sam, aware of his passion for racing. Sam was thrilled to have this opportunity and was inspired by the level of interest from people who had never been exposed to the idea of Biblical applications in the business world.

At the end of the seminar, Sam was approached by a man who at that time was a notable championship driver and team owner. He asked Sam if he would consider taking over his race team and incorporating the Biblical principles as a testimony in the world of professional racing. What a request . . . what an opportunity . . . yet, this would be a huge leap of faith to venture into a new arena of work, life, and trust.

Chapter 9

PAIN AND BETRAYAL

ONCE AGAIN, SAM WALKED INTO our neatly packaged little world with the excitement of a child on Christmas morning, enthusiastically telling me about the seminar and the job offer. He saw this as a tremendous ministry opportunity for him to invest in the lives of individuals who didn't have the opportunity to become involved in a church or Bible study group. We prayed a lot about this huge decision. After several months, we sold our dental labs and our home and moved to Charlotte, North Carolina. Sam immediately started Bible studies in the race shop, and many of our team members made commitments to Christ. Remarkable testimonies of people coming to Christ came about over the next three years.

Sam and I both learned to love the racing community and began teaching Bible studies and serving on the Board of Motor Racing Outreach, a unique ministry within the world of professional auto racing. With 29 race weekends each year, along with other testing dates and more, this was a complete lifestyle change for us. We enjoyed the travel as Sam attended every race and test, and Kevin was part of the race-day crew every weekend. Christen was now attending a Christian university, and

Kevin was continuing with his home studies.

After three wonderful years of working with the race team, changes were made that caused Sam to feel he should resign. We had moved to Charlotte with a desire to glorify God in every aspect of managing the race team and to be a testimony to lift up the name of Jesus. We made plans to resign, confident that God was leading us.

We prayed about our decision, and with the resources we had in the bank, we felt we could trust God to provide. If God didn't provide a job quickly, we could go for quite a while before we'd notice the lack of income. We really weren't concerned, as during those three years other race teams had made many offers to Sam. Sam resigned, and immediately our phone started ringing. He was to start working with another team within days.

When Sam showed up at his new job, his employers met him at the door to tell him they'd changed their minds and didn't need him. Over the next three months, he received many calls and got hired many times, only to show up and be told over and over that they didn't want him after all. We could not figure out what was happening. Sam had a stellar reputation, and his record as a team manager was exceptional.

We continued to say we were trusting God. I knew we had that cushion in the bank, making it quite easy to declare that everything we had belonged to God. However, if it truly does, and we actually mean it, we need to realize that He has the right to take it just as much as He has the right to provide it.

After three months of unemployment, we received

one of those formidable certified letters from the IRS. They had discovered a mistake on our tax return following the sale of our business three years earlier. (I'm still amazed at the difference one decimal point can make when you have trusted your CPA to carefully file everything.) In this letter, we were told we owed a huge sum of additional taxes to the IRS, along with compounded penalties and interest that had been applied over the three-year period. The IRS placed liens on everything we owned and gave us a 60-day time limit to pay it all in full. Repeated calls, conversations, and requests proved that they would not consider negotiating, and all liens would remain in place until the debt was paid in full.

While driving to the bank to obtain a certified check that would use almost our entire savings cushion, my car engine blew, and I found myself stranded along the interstate. It was not a good day. Hours later, when I finally got home, I discovered the dog had chewed up Kevin's mouth-guard retainer and the pump on the water filter had just burned up. We still had no income and had sent most of our financial cushion to the IRS. Trusting God just got a little harder!

When I could sort of figure things out and hold on to some form of security and control, I had found it quite easy to make all sorts of proclamations concerning our trusting the Lord. As long as I knew I had some crackers in my purse, I'd smile and tell everyone we were trusting God. As I was faced with these new financial challenges, I was reminded of the conversation that Jesus had with

Peter when Jesus asked him: "Do you love me? Do you really love me?" It felt like God was saying to me: "Do you trust me, Ann? Do you really trust me?"

I absolutely wanted to faithfully trust God, but I'll admit that as time went on, it became harder and harder. When my narrative of trusting God carried with it an expectation of what God should do, was I truly trusting Him?

One day a dear friend called Sam to let him know that the man who had replaced him at the race team was spreading incredible stories and lies about Sam throughout the racing community. When that man heard that a team had hired Sam, he would immediately call them with incredulous tales of Sam pilfering tens of thousands of dollars in money and equipment from the team. This man completely attacked Sam's integrity and reputation with false allegations. We had no idea why he would do that, but word had traveled quickly throughout the tightly knit racing community.

It was an extremely hard time for me to sit by and watch people we had loved, respected, and ministered to believe the lies about my husband. I wanted to fight for his character and reputation. Our only reason for moving to Charlotte was to lift up the name of Jesus, to do what we felt God had called us to do. I was angry, but Sam would not fight back. He knew he had done nothing wrong and had never taken one cent from the team. He said our part was to pray as he claimed every verse in the Bible that says God will be our defense if we will allow Him to be. He claimed the promise of Psalm 91:2: "You are my defender and protector. You are my God; in you I trust."

By the end of our fourth month, after sending our financial cushion to the IRS, we had $200 left in the bank and still no prospect of a job. I felt like God had taken away our security blanket and all of my crackers and was saying, "Trust Me."

Sam and I went from "having it all" to total dependence on God. Over the years, we had collected a lot of "toys" and junk in our lives, so for the next few months we financially survived by selling the toys we had accumulated. In de-junking our lives, we experienced an amazing blessing! We found a sense of peace and freedom, but ... Sam still didn't have a job.

During all these months, Sam made calls daily and constantly handed out resumes, but the days rolled into weeks and the weeks into months. We began to experience discouragement, depression, and even some anger toward God. I would remind God of how faithful we'd been: We'd trusted Him. Sam had taught seminars and Bible studies. We'd walked with Him a long time, and we were in this for the long haul! It felt like God had mixed our life up with someone else's. I recognized I was trying to impress God with all of our service to Him, but we had been faithful! *Isn't that how this Christian walk works?*

If I was going to trust God to keep His promises, I needed to understand the promises He'd made. I was hurting and I had a lot of questions. I was trusting God, but I was also angry that we had prayed about our decisions and ended up where we were.

If I was angry—and I was—I realized that I did not think God had done His part, which implied that God was supposed to come through for me. I didn't want to think that way, but Jesus had promised an abundant life. *So what did that really mean? My life looked more like cracker crumbs than filet mignon at this point, so what was I missing?* I was entering a new season of learning what trust and the abundant life actually looked like.

I learned that if I believe that God is obligated to act or grant every request I make (well, at least the big ones), then I set myself up to be disappointed by God. I was beginning to understand that true trust doesn't mean that God follows the script of my expectations. I began searching scripture for God's promises. Isaiah 41:13 became a balm to my hurting and discouraged soul: "For I am the Lord your God who takes hold of your right hand and says to you, Do not fear; I will help you."

After several months had passed, Sam began taking odd jobs, and I do mean odd jobs. Talk about brokenness! Here was a man who had started and owned seven corporations, led a successful NASCAR race team, and taught hundreds of corporate leaders how to run their businesses. I'll never forget the day I watched him selling race programs at one of the largest races of the year at the entrance to the racetrack for $5 an hour. This was the man who just months before was sitting on top of the pit box on pit lane overseeing a multimillion-dollar racing organization. My admiration and respect for Sam Conway soared that day as he humbly sold those programs with a smile to enable us to pay our bills! We had gone from owning nice cars, a boat, partnership in an airplane, and having most anything we wanted to being thankful for basic transportation. I now know that we were right where God wanted us. We were depending on Him and Him alone!

Chapter 10

A JOB FOR ME AND NOT FOR THEE?

As SAM AND I ATTEMPTED to discern what God's plans for us were, I decided to resign from my voluntary position on the Board of Motor Racing Outreach due to all of the rumors circulating about Sam. He wouldn't consider resigning, since he had not done any of the things of which he was being accused, but I had had enough. I went to the next board meeting armed with my prepared resignation speech; however, they started the meeting by announcing the need to immediately hire an administrative assistant and needed the board's approval. At that moment, it was as if God tapped me on the shoulder and said, "You're it!" I actually looked around and behind me, as the message almost seemed audible.

I couldn't believe it! I sat in that meeting dumbfounded. There was NO WAY! God simply would not do this to me! I had been a full-time, stay-at-home mom since Christen was born, and Kevin still had at least two more years of high school. *How would that work?* I was convinced that God had gotten our prayers mixed up—He was supposed to get *Sam* a job, not me!

I somehow endured the board meeting, listening to

their discussion concerning the rumors circulating about Sam, confident that God would and could receive glory through it all. Although I still had my doubts, I decided to remain on the board.

I was truly shaken by what had happened at the meeting, because I knew that the job had my name on it. I had all of the qualifications of the individual they were looking for. I was even hesitant to tell Sam about it when I got home. When I finally told him, we agreed that I should go as a temp to fill in only until he found a job, which should happen very soon.

The biggest problem was Kevin. He was in the tenth grade, and that meant Sam would have to be his teacher for the remainder of the school year if I went to work, teaching Biology, Advanced Math, English Literature, and other courses. Sam said he was up to the challenge and would enjoy teaching Kevin, although I was sure he had no idea what all it entailed!

The CEO of the ministry was thrilled when I called and told him I was willing to work on a temporary basis until they could find whom they were looking for. He wanted me to begin immediately.

It was very hard for me to enter the working world as a full-time employee. The first week, I cried all the way to and from work. (My coworkers all just thought I had severe allergies.) I would crank up praise and worship music on the car radio and pray all the way, asking God to help me make it through the day … and to please, please get Sam a job! I quoted every scripture I could remember: Philippians 4:13: "I can do all things through

Christ who strengthens me" and Romans 8:28: "And we know that all things work together for good to them that love God and are called according to His purpose." I loved God and believed I was following what I knew to be His will at the time, but I sure couldn't see any good coming out of me having a full-time job.

On Sam and Kevin's first day of schooling together, I had lesson plans, assignments, and tests for Kevin's studies prepared and ready for Sam. I was concerned but hoped they'd have a successful start. When I returned that evening I found them in the garage preparing one of Kevin's race cars for an upcoming race, only to discover they hadn't touched any schoolwork that day.

That evening I explained to Sam the importance of sticking to Kevin's study schedule before working on the car. They appeared to do a little better for a couple of days, but then I came home to a day of them working in the garage again.

At the time, Kevin was taking an Advanced Math course via video instruction and had always complained that the video teacher was boring. It seemed it had taken Sam only 10 minutes of watching that video to agree and to decide that Kevin could learn more physics and geometry on a race car than by listening to some guy on a video. They explained to me they were in the garage for math class.

I could see this wasn't working on any level and once again pleaded with Sam to stick to the lesson plans and schedule. He said he agreed with Kevin that it was extremely boring.

Leaving each morning was absolute torture for me. The job itself was fine; however, the pay was minimal, and my concern for Kevin's education was constant. Fortunately, Sam was still focused on finding a job. Returning home on day five, they greeted me outside with sheepish grins on their faces. I knew they had been up to something. I stepped out of the car and said: "Okay. Go ahead and tell me, because I can tell you two have been scheming something today."

Sam went on to explain that over the past few days he had come to realize how intelligent Kevin was, so they had gone to the local community college, where Sam had asked to see the chancellor and had convinced him to give Kevin an entrance exam. Sam proudly announced that the chancellor had agreed, and Kevin had aced the exam!

The chancellor said that a new semester was beginning in two days, and they would welcome Kevin. Both Kevin and Sam were ecstatic! It all sounded wonderful to them, and since Kevin was a full-time resident in the area, all he had to do was to show up in two days with only $400 to begin his studies. *Kevin was to begin college, and he was only 15 years old!*

A year ago, $400 would have been pocket change, but that was more than I was bringing home in a week, and there were innumerable bills to pay. There was no way we could ever come up with $400 in two days. We'd already sold everything we could sell.

I went to work the next day with a heavy heart, knowing we did not have the money and knowing how disappointed Kevin would be. Sam wasn't a bit concerned. He believed that God would somehow provide it. I just wasn't so sure.

Upon returning from work that evening, Kevin and Sam were ready to go to church for a special service and were surprised when I told them I wasn't going. I was too depressed to go and a bit unhappy that God was now messing with Kevin. It was bad enough that Sam and I had to go through all of this, but now Kevin actually believed he was starting college in just 24 hours. And if he didn't, it was obvious Sam's home education system would never work. As I walked out to the car with them, I grabbed the mail and waved goodbye. I just wanted them to leave so I could have my own private pity-party. Nothing was going as it should!

I walked into our bedroom and tossed the mail on the bed. I then threw myself across it and began to sob my heart out. I told God how disappointed I was. I knew He already knew it, but it somehow helped me to tell Him. I also told Him how I wanted to be obedient to Him and that I did trust Him, but sometimes trusting was just hard and so unnatural. I had learned in the past how God and not my circumstances were the source of true joy, and I acknowledged that He was enlarging my capacity to know and love and trust Him. "But God," I cried, "this is not an easy journey You've given us!"

Once again I felt that gentle prompting: "Do you trust me, Ann? Do you really, really trust Me? Remember, I have come that you might have Abundant Life." I dried my tears and decided to look at the mail, confident that it would only be more bills. There was an envelope addressed to us from a couple whom we'd met two years earlier at a business seminar Sam had taught for individuals going through bankruptcy. They were there because they had lost everything. They even had watched their beautiful home auctioned off on the courthouse steps.

When I saw their names on the envelope, I thought, *What in the world could they want with us? They're even poorer than we are!* I opened the envelope and discovered a check for $400 with a sticky-note on it that said: "Don't know what's going on in your life, but God told us to send this to you! Love in Jesus."

I fell to my knees and asked God's forgiveness for my lack of faith and trust. I wanted to throw away any remaining packets of crackers I had. I couldn't stop praising Him! I thanked Him for the faithfulness of those dear Christian friends who had followed God's lead that very day and sent the money; one day later would have been too late for Kevin to get into that semester. I'm sure that those precious people needed that money as much as we did; however, their gift was such a blessing to us, and they later felt equally blessed when we called to tell them of the timing of their obedience.

That was the only time we ever received unexpected money during our unemployment journey; however, I could tell you of time after time when God met our every need. God cares, and He cared about everything that was touching our lives. I have found that God is always in the details and He is never early and never late.

God allowed Sam to be without work for over two

years—more than two years of odd jobs, interviews, and resumes. God allowed me to serve as a "temp" for those two years. Only God knows why we had to walk this path, yet He taught us so very much during that time. It wasn't fun and was often difficult, but we learned so much about ourselves and our walk with Christ. God used that time to teach us that our identity doesn't come from what we do or what we think about ourselves or through anyone else's approval; it comes from God and God alone.

First Thessalonians 5:18 says, "In all things give thanks, for this is the will of God in Christ Jesus concerning you." Paul didn't say to give thanks for all things, but in all things. I was beginning to see that when I relinquished my will to Him and gave Him my total trust— when I got rid of my crackers, I experienced the Abundant Life He promised.

During our time of unemployment, Kevin started his own business in our garage, setting up race cars for competitors. Sam had to drive Kevin to college because he was only 15 years old and didn't have a driver's license. Yet Kevin was working on very expensive cars that belonged to race teams, and on the weekends he was racing on tracks at over 100 mph.

As soon as Kevin turned 16, he used the money he had saved to buy a used black Nissan Pathfinder. It seemed I was always following him, driving behind that vehicle with the spare tire on the back that said *Pathfinder* to pick up or drop something off. When Kevin saved enough money to buy a newer vehicle, we bought his

Pathfinder ... another detail in God's timetable that we would later discover.

The day came when Sam's reputation was totally restored within the racing community by his willingness to stand firm in living the Christian life before them. Multiple individuals came to ask forgiveness for believing the lies. Opportunities opened for him to counsel others, and friendships were restored. During his two years of unemployment, Sam continued to lead many Bible studies within the racing community, and God opened ministry opportunities we never expected.

During this time, Kevin so excelled at the community college that he transferred to the University of North Carolina after one semester. He advanced in his racing career and won the championship in the Legends Car Series and was also racing late models as God continued to provide sponsorships for his racing career.

Christen dropped out of the university she was attending and moved back home as a very different young woman than the one we had sent to college. Disillusioned with the educational system, jobs, friends, church, and life itself, she was on a new search for the meaning of life, and it wasn't an easy road for her or us.

After two years of unemployment, Larry Burkett asked Sam if he would consider coming on staff at Christian Financial Concepts as Vice President of Marketing and Product Development. After much prayer, we once again placed our home on the market and moved to Gainesville, Georgia.

Christen had moved into a house with a roommate

and was working, although she was admittedly miserable in her various jobs. Kevin was continuing his studies at UNC, working with a marketing firm and moving up in the various racing series. Leaving both of them in Charlotte and moving the four hours away was a challenge, but we knew we could entrust them to God's care.

Chapter 11

HEARTBREAK AND CONFUSION

AS A YOUNG TEEN, Christen was happy and was zealous in her devotion to learning God's Word and sharing it with others. She had a heart that naturally reached out to others, especially the underdog. From the time she was young, Christen had put a high value on justice, and when life didn't make sense to her, she went to battle to right the wrong.

As Christen moved into her later teen years, her zeal for "justice for all" became even stronger. I had always admired her nonjudgmental attitude and willingness to accept those whom she perceived the church had "turned its back on" or were being "shunned." However, as we all know, one's perceptions become one's reality, and Christen began to feel it was her responsibility to reach out to show the "most misunderstood segment of society" the love of Jesus. In her earnestness to reach out to the ones whom she felt had been overlooked by the church, she began making friendships and relationships with people who were much older, bitter at life, mad at God, and wounded and broken by life experiences.

The more of herself and her time that she invested in righting the social wrongs of the church, the more I could see it taking its toll in her own life. She was sincere in her undertaking; however, she also was totally unprepared and not mature enough to handle the individuals who were thrilled with her efforts to help them. I could see that this was overwhelming Christen and beginning to negatively influence her, as well as her relationship with the Lord and us, as she began to internalize the problems, perspectives, and attitudes of the ones she set out to help. However, it was impossible to enable her to see what was happening in her own life as a result.

I loved the fact that we had been close. One thing about being so close is that you notice small changes. It was little things at first—things hardly worth mentioning, but I could tell she was thinking about more than she was sharing.

The years when Christen struggled became hard years for Sam and me. Our relationship with her was never completely severed, but it was strained about as far as it could be strained. We loved our daughter, but we struggled with her life choices. We didn't understand where we had failed her or how she could have chosen the path she chose. We were at times angry with God, disappointed with her, guilt-ridden, and grief-stricken.

We also realized we had both grown in our faith. We had recognized legalism for what it was and saw how pathetic our earlier view of God had been. We had lived the performance-based formula for the type of Christian life that we had been taught. God was in the process of teaching us what the relational, abundant life with Christ actually looked like. We often discussed what simply being a Christ-follower meant, and it was nothing like the religious rules we once had believed were so important.

With our new insight, we asked Christen's forgiveness for the years of implementing in our home rules that had no true Biblical basis. In love, we had acted on what we had been taught and had believed—at that time—to be good and true. We had focused on the "rules," thinking it was for our children's good. Later, we realized it actually was a formula that left no room for grace or true freedom in Christ.

During Christen's college years, she began making choices that took her further and further away from the principles she had been taught and had once enthusiastically lived by. She began to defy everything for which she knew God's Word stood, thus creating a life cycle of failures, depression, and total misery. Now she was not only defiant but also angry and bitter. Nothing in her life seemed to bring her joy.

We tried to show her unconditional love. Her words and behavior did not make that easy. Some days it was impossible without God's love. Her defiant rebellion tested us in inconceivable ways, but we hung on to God's promise that she was His and He loved her even more than we did. Christen had always walked to the beat of a different drummer, enjoying the shock value of her choices. Now, however, everything she said and did felt like a personal attack on anything her father and I stood for.

When Christen left college, she moved back into our

home. We would set aside time to have lunch together and try to do things Christen would enjoy. When we later moved to Georgia, she did not move with us, and we spoke on the phone regularly, but we knew she was slipping away from us. We felt a veil—not a wall—just a disquieting veil coming between us. Over time, Christen changed into a person we did not know.

Fear of losing my beautiful daughter engulfed me. All I wanted was for her to be happy and live a life pleasing to God. She was making choices that would do neither. I searched the scripture for answers, but I did not know what to do. I was watching Christen lose touch with her own self and saw her walking away from us and from God. We knew only God could change her heart, but it is a horrible and powerless feeling to watch your child on this downward spiral, going deeper and deeper with each passing day, and to be rejected with every word you say to her. All we could do was reaffirm our love to her and trust God.

Chapter 12

DISCOVERING THE DREAMER

SAM AND I BOTH WORKED at the Christian Financial Concepts ministry in Georgia and enjoyed our new friendships and the challenge of new jobs. It was difficult to leave my children in Charlotte, even though I realized they were growing up. Sam and I believed we had trained them to make good choices and prayed daily that they would. Kevin was thriving with college, racing, and a job with a marketing firm. It was much harder for us to leave Christen because of all the uncertainty in her life. We continued to entrust them to God and thanked Him for both of our children.

We had almost daily communication with both Christen and Kevin after we moved. Every week, we made the four-hour drive to Charlotte to attend Kevin's races. On occasion, Christen would join us, but more often than not she said she didn't have time to see us. On those occasions, we would stop by where she was working for just a quick hug and to tell her we loved her. Many times we did not feel our love was reciprocated, but we continued to trust God.

One morning at 2:30 a.m., our phone rang. My heart pounded and my mind immediately kicked into high gear, imagining every possible worst-case scenario. "This is Dr. Clark from the Behavioral Health Care Center in Charlotte," a man's voice told us. "We have your daughter Christen here. Fearing her suicidal behavior, some friends dropped her off a couple hours ago. She is currently on a suicide watch and will be having psychiatric evaluations later this morning. She wanted us to let you know."

We immediately got dressed and headed to Charlotte. Upon arrival at the Center, we were told that Christen had sat with a loaded pistol pointed to the roof of her mouth for two hours before her friends could wrestle the gun from her hand. She told them she had decided she did not want to live any longer. Her life felt hopeless: every job had fallen apart, she had debts she could not repay, and every relationship in her life was a disaster.

Later that day we talked with a doctor who gave us some encouragement. She told us one thing was very clear after talking with and evaluating Christen: she loved us dearly and deeply. We were also encouraged when we were able to visit with Christen that afternoon, and she was very happy to see us. She was required to stay at the Center for a couple of weeks for counseling, but we could call her every day, which we did. We also made several trips to see her while she was there.

At the end of her stay, the counselors consulted and agreed that she had come to terms with her many issues and was ready to move forward. We asked her to consider coming to Georgia to live with us. It would give her a fresh start with a new location, friends, and job. She promised us that she would consider our invitation.

Two weeks later Christen called and said there was nothing left for her in Charlotte. We drove up on the following day and helped her move out of her apartment and into our home in Georgia, storing everything in our garage. She occupied the upstairs floor of our new home, and we were thrilled.

Christen made friends easily, but it wasn't long before she made the same type of friendships and relationships she had left in Charlotte. Her defiant attitude returned and was reflected in every area of her life. She bitterly complained that nothing ever worked out for her!

Sam and I tried to be unmovable and unshakable in reaching out to her with love, but it was not easy. One day she looked her dad in the eye and told him she was against everything he stood for. She did not agree with or embrace any of the principles she had been taught as a child. Sam stood up, walked to her, wrapped his arms around her, and looked her in the eye. He quietly said: "There is nothing you can ever say or do that will change my love for you. I may not agree with your life choices, but I will always love you."

That was the beginning of a very small turnaround in her life. I can't tell you it was easy, because it wasn't. She broke our hearts over and over as we reached out to her. We stood on God's Word and entrusted her totally to His care, knowing there was nothing we could do to change her heart.

Once again I was faced with trusting God, believing I could trust Him completely. Although it felt like all of my hopes and dreams for Christen had been shattered, I looked to God to both redeem her life and work on mine. I clung to Micah 7:7: "But as for me, I watch in hope for the Lord, I wait for God my Savior; my God will hear me." I knew Christen was God's child and that He would pursue her just as the shepherd left the ninety-nine to go after that one lost sheep. I laid Christen at the feet of Jesus.

One morning as I was sitting at my desk at the ministry, a coworker slipped his head around the corner and tossed me a book. "You should read this," he said. "It helped my wife and me. We now have a better understanding about what was going on in our son's life." The title was *Strong-Willed Child or Dreamer?* I immediately was reminded of the many books I'd read over the years concerning the strong-willed child. We had implemented every imaginable recommendation to no avail. I thanked him for the book, figuring I'd skim over it that evening to please him.

That night, after reading only the first few pages, I became captivated by the description of what the author called the dreamer child. It was as if a veil was being lifted from my eyes as I realized someone was finally describing my daughter. This book also described our life with our daughter. I devoured each page as I read what her perception of her own life might look like and how we were possibly being perceived by her. I was overwhelmed! *Could it be that all the things I had supposed were rebellion or disrespect merely resulted from the way God had wired her?* I couldn't stop reading. This author had such an understanding of Christen's personality. According to what I read, we had done absolutely everything wrong for her to feel affirmation, acceptance, and unconditional love from us.

The book was both enlightening and heart-wrenching at the same time. Each page was untangling, exposing, and illuminating a new revelation of who Christen actually was and who she could become. It dismantled and magnified the various misguided ways we had tried to deal with her, thinking of her as a strong-willed child. Having been distracted by all of the mainstream teaching on strong-willed children, we had failed to embrace the amazing and unique qualities God had granted to Christen.

I read the entire book that evening and was over-whelmed and consumed with deep grief. Our lack of understanding and our communication with Christen had undeniably been the opposite of what she had needed.

After I completed the book, I began reflecting on Christen's life through the lens of this book. I remem-bered those early years of her wanting to play the piano and enrolling her into a Suzuki piano course. After several lessons, the instructor had come to me and told me that it was obvious Christen was not a good fit for learning via that method.

The Suzuki method uses a constant-repetition-of-song technique before exposure to note-reading, but Christen did not want to play "Twinkle, Twinkle, Little Star" without knowing why one note should be held longer than another. She was only 5 years old, but she challenged the teacher repeatedly, asking, "Why?" Christen wanted to understand how that teacher knew how long a note should be held. The answer that it "was just the way we sing it" wasn't a satisfactory explanation for Christen. She wanted proof. "Just because I said so" was also never an acceptable answer for Christen.

Once we put her in a traditional piano course, where she could see notes, timing, etc. she excelled in her piano skills.

That was just one small example of how Christen had walked through every day of her life. She questioned everything and needed truthful and complete answers. Her perceptions were so sharp that she could spot a phony immediately and really didn't have time for phonies. She was intuitive and easily bored in a classroom setting. When she was young and questioned us or her teachers in search of valid answers, she often had been reprimanded for questioning authority.

I began to see my daughter differently as I realized how she had been wired by God. All of her life, without considering that she could be wired differently, I had responded to her through the lens of *my* perceptions. I am a born follower. I enjoy boundaries and parameters. All my daddy ever had to say to me regarding a rule is that it was there because he said so. That was good enough for me. However, when we tried to set boundaries with Christen, she would want to know *why*. We saw her need for an explanation as defiance or evidence of being strong-willed. Sam was better with her, usually trying to offer an explanation, which would lead to me becoming annoyed with him and her. I told him that giving her all of those explanations was undermining his authority. After reading the book, I was devastated; I realized how flawed my past parenting skills had been in regard to this precious daughter.

Another realization I gleaned from the book involved our conflicts with Christen over the rules and behaviors associated with being a Christian. Christen got in trouble because she challenged all of them. Looking back, however, I realized they needed to be challenged.

God has opened my eyes to the legalism that I had easily embraced when I was young. The message I had believed was that we are saved by God's grace, *but* we have to behave a certain way or follow certain rules to *stay* in God's favor. Righteousness became *our* responsibility, and God was to respond in almost an obligatory manner.

I spent a lot of time that night and into the early morning hours talking to God about all that I had discovered and all that had been revealed to me through that book. All I could do was trust God for discernment and guidance as I wrestled to untangle and dismantle my part in Christen's downward spiral. I tried to rest in the couple of hours that remained before going to work.

I had coffee brewing at daybreak, as I could hardly wait for Sam to wake up to share the transformational information I had just learned. The minute he opened his eyes, I placed a cup of coffee and the book in his hands. He looked at the cover and said, "Oh, I know that author—he lives right here in Atlanta." I asked Sam to call him as soon as we got to the office.

When we arrived at work, I went straight into Sam's office, and he called Dr. Ron Braund. Obviously Dr. Braund wasn't easily accessible to random callers, but I listened as my amazing husband negotiated, and within minutes Dr. Braund was on the line. Sam simply said "hello" and handed me the phone. I wasn't expecting that, so I had no idea what to say to him, other than the fact that I had just read his book and he was the first one to ever understand my daughter and I wanted him to see her.

Dr. Braund was extremely courteous but quickly explained that he did not do one-on-one counseling any longer but would be more than happy to direct her to a competent counselor, as long as she herself was seeking it. I explained that she wasn't and likely wouldn't, but that I just knew he was the one who could reach her. As I feared losing the one person in the world who could possibly get through to Christen, I was crying rather hysterically.

He suggested that she read the book and if she felt a need for counseling to call back. Since I feared she'd be resistant to any book that I suggested, I asked his advice for getting her to read it. He chuckled and said that if she were a true dreamer, the only way to get her to read the book would be for me to tell her that I wanted her opinion because I was unsure of its validity. "Dreamers love to give their opinion," he said, "especially if the one asking is unsure of where they stand on the content."

I was discouraged when I learned that he wouldn't see her. *Didn't he hear the desperation in my voice?* Almost everything in her world was continuing to fall apart—she needed counseling from this man who understood her! However, I had to be content with the possibility of her reading the book.

That very evening, when Christen got home from work I had the book lying on the counter. She picked it up and asked what it was. I replied that it was something someone had given me to read, but I wasn't sure how I felt about it and would really appreciate her opinion. She immediately said, "Sure, let me read it."

She walked to the family room, stretched out on the sofa, and began to read. Within thirty minutes she called out, "This guy knows me!" A little later she said "I think this guy has been following me around. Do you think he's been hiding in our house?"

I purposely stayed out of the room as she continued to read … Like me, she read the entire book that night.

When she finished, she came to me and said: "Tell Daddy I want him to find this author. No matter how long it takes, I want to talk to him. He's the first person that's ever understood me." She knew that Sam had a great "knack" for locating people and opening doors to meet them, so I picked up the book and as naively as I could asked who the author was, to which she responded, "I have no idea, but I need to meet him."

Needless to say, Sam and I called Dr. Braund first thing the next morning. After much discussion and more tears, he agreed to meet with her, assess her, and then determine the proper counselor referral for her. Within a week, Christen met with him, and when she returned home we asked no questions at all. She simply stated that she was going back the next week for another session. We didn't comment, but we were thrilled.

After several counseling sessions with Christen, Dr. Braund requested that Sam and I come in for a session with her. At that time, many things were discussed and many issues were addressed, but nothing felt earth-shattering. We felt a small sense of relief that Christen wasn't blaming all of her problems on Sam and me, in spite of the fact that we truly had contributed in many areas out of pure ignorance on how God had wired her.

Dr. Braund suggested that Christen consider moving out of our home and into a place of her own now that she had a job that enabled her to do that. She found a small rental just 6 miles from us, and we helped her settle in. She loved it. We began to see small changes in her life. She began reading good books by C. S. Lewis and other Christian authors. Amazingly, she even wanted to discuss them with us!

We stood in awe as we slowly watched her hardened heart soften toward spiritual things. There was never a huge lightning-strike moment or supercharged event that happened. It was just a sloturning of her attitudes and interests. She stopped by our home often, doing her laundry, eating, or just visiting with us. She and I would meet during our lunch hour three or four times a week, and we became friends again.

Sam and I were thrilled with the transformation and

answered prayers we were seeing both in Christen and in ourselves. We realized we were responding to her differently as we began to understand how a dreamer is wired and that a dreamer sees everything that happens as if it is somehow related to the other person's intentions toward her. We now understood that dreamers are the most imaginative, sensitive, and idealistic of all personalities, always looking for true authenticity. As a result of being so idealistic and setting such high standards—that no one can attain—many times they feel let down and abandoned by the people who love them the most.

I'll never forget the second and last session that Sam and I participated in with Christen and Dr. Braund. It will be branded in my mind and heart for all my years on this earth. As we discussed past hurts and offenses, those both previously known and unknown, between Christen and us; asking forgiveness where and when needed; and addressing areas where we had been wrong and had misgivings about each other, the session ended with Dr. Braund asking each of us if we felt we had any unfinished issues between us. A period of quietness followed, with each of us having the same response: amazingly, we had no unfinished issues between us. Little did I realize how those words would comfort this mother's heart in just a few short months.

Chapter 13

THE MYSTERIOUS PATHFINDER

LIFE IN GEORGIA WAS GOOD. We were grateful to God for returning our daughter to us. Christen excelled in her new job and had been promoted to a management position. On the Sundays when she wasn't working, she often attended church with us. Kevin continued working between classes and studying toward earning his degree at UNC as his racing career advanced into the higher series.

Sam and I were both enjoying our jobs at the ministry. On weekday mornings, we would drive to work in separate cars, because our jobs often took us out of the office. As I followed Sam's black Pathfinder to work, I remembered thinking that I had logged almost five years of travel time following it. I thanked God for the degree of normalcy to which our life had returned.

As Thanksgiving approached, Christen began experiencing sharp pain in her lower left abdominal area that would drive her to her knees. Her doctor gave her a prescription for pain medication, but it did not give her any relief. Numerous office exams, sonograms, and scans of her abdominal area revealed no abnormalities. She hated missing work, but the pain became intolerable, even incapacitating. She would double over in agony, sometimes throwing up as the pain intensified. After three weeks on the maximum amount of painkillers (which were not relieving the pain), the doctor decided to do laparoscopic exploratory surgery to see if they could formulate a diagnosis.

I went with Christen to the surgeon's office. He explained the surgery and assured us that this was an extremely routine procedure that he performed multiple times a day, several days a week.

It was one week before Christmas when Sam and I picked Christen up at 5 a.m. to take her to the hospital. After she was prepped for surgery, Sam and I were allowed to see her. Sam prayed for her and for the surgery. I'll never forget being a little embarrassed when the surgeon came in and Christen wagged her finger at him and said, "Whatever you do, do not take out my appendix or my gallbladder if you don't have to." I was shocked by her abrupt manner, asking her why she would say that. She replied: "Oh, Mom, they do that all the time! I just don't want him to take mine."

With a last-minute hug, we all said we loved each other, and she was whisked off. Sam and I were led to the surgical waiting area.

It wasn't too long before the surgeon came out to tell us that he had not found anything unusual or abnormal that would cause her pain. He then added that he had removed her gallbladder and appendix, with the flippant comment that no one needs them anyway, saying, "It will save her from having problems with them in the future." Without further conversation, he turned and walked away.

The medical staff was having trouble stabilizing Christen's blood pressure and oxygen levels. Many hours passed before they finally said we could take her to our home. However, once home, Christen's pain intensified, and after a fitful night on much pain medication, I called the doctor's office the minute they opened. I described what Christen's night had been like and asked to speak to the surgeon. They explained to me that Christen's pain was normal: she not only still had her original pain but now would have the pain associated with laparoscopic surgery due to the trapped gas that could move around in her body. After all, she was now also recovering from an appendectomy as well as gallbladder surgery.

They said that I should expect the pain to become a little worse over the next couple of days, but then she could expect relief. I continued administering the pain medications as directed.

At times her pain would become so intense I could barely stand to watch her suffer. Throughout the day I called the surgeon's office every couple of hours, pleading with the young-sounding voice on the phone to please let me speak to a nurse or the doctor. I asked if I could bring her to the office or take her to the hospital. The girl would place me on hold and come back with the same explanation each time: "Mrs. Conway, this amount of pain is 100% normal and will not let up for at least another 24 to 48 hours." She accused Christen of being a drama queen and me an overbearing mother. She told me I needed to stop calling them.

I did not stop calling. I called them eight times that day, begging them for help. When I described her distended abdomen and its bluish color, I was told that was completely normal. There are no words to describe what the following night was like for Christen and the pain level she experienced. Neither Sam nor I slept. We stayed right by Christen's side, praying for relief from the pain and wisdom to help our daughter. Having gotten no sleep that night, Sam had to leave the house at 4:30 a.m. for a flight to Philadelphia, where he was the featured speaker at a corporate Christmas luncheon for several hundred businessmen. He had booked a flight to return by midnight that same day.

He quietly prayed with Christen before leaving the house. I remember standing on the porch in the darkness of the early morning hours waving goodbye. I knew Sam hated to leave, but this speaking engagement had been scheduled for more than eight months. He felt obligated to go and would return home later that same night.

Christen and I were in our family room. I had put on some relaxing music and turned on the Christmas tree lights as she continually tried to get comfortable in the big recliner. We watched the tree lights flickering as I talked her through some breathing techniques in an attempt to help calm her and lessen the pain. Nothing made it easier for her, and I felt totally helpless.

At exactly 8 a.m., when I knew the doctor's office would open, I called. This time I was completely done with pleading and begging and demanded that someone see my daughter immediately. I was placed on hold for almost 15 minutes. The girl came back and said that I could take Christen to a certain hospital near Atlanta where the doctor was doing surgery all morning. She instructed me to simply take her to the Emergency Room, and the surgeon would be notified that we were there. Whenever he finished his surgeries for that day, he would then see her. She emphasized that I might have to wait there for hours, but eventually he would have a look at her.

As uncaring as she sounded, I agreed to follow that plan. At least in a hospital there would be doctors and nurses to see Christen's pain level. She could be monitored, and I hoped her pain would be treated in an Emergency Room.

We quickly got dressed and got into the car. As Christen reclined the front passenger seat, I realized I had no idea where this hospital was, except that it was 45 miles from our house. Christen said she knew where it was, and off we went.

As I turned onto the interstate that morning, just days before Christmas, traffic was barely moving. We were inching along at 15–20 mph, and all lanes were totally gridlocked. At times we were not moving at all. Beside me, Christen said: "It kind of feels hard to breathe. Please pray for me." I placed my hand on her thigh and began praying out loud, simply asking God to help her and to please help us get to the hospital.

All I could see ahead was bumper-to-bumper traffic. I was afraid this trip could take us a very long time. Each time my praying ended, she would say, "Pray again, Mama; pray again," and I would.

I stopped praying to grab my cell phone and dial the doctor's office. I asked them if they had alerted the Emergency Room that we were on our way. The same girl replied: "No, because you are only going there to wait on the doctor. There is no need to notify them."

I hung up and found the direct number to the hospital Emergency Room, dialed the number, and was able to speak to the triage nurse. I explained that I was on my way there with my daughter, but we were caught in traffic; I described Christen's symptoms. That was the first time I felt anyone expressed a positive response to my concerns. The triage nurse assured me they would be watching and waiting for us to get there.

"Pray again, Mama," Christen said the second I hung up. I continued to pray out loud for Christen.

Although I had a sense of urgency, I was not driving in apprehension of impending peril. In my heart I was silently screaming for God's help. Our immediate need was to quickly get her to that hospital so they could help her. After speaking with that nurse, I was now heading toward someone who seemed to care.

We continued to inch along the interstate until out of nowhere a black Pathfinder managed to squeeze between my front bumper and the car in front of me. Suddenly, it swerved onto the right shoulder of the road. Without hesitation, I locked my eyes on the spare tire cover that said *Pathfinder* and followed it onto the shoulder.

We gained speed as we raced by gridlocked cars, and

I could feel my hands tightening around the steering wheel. As the glaring morning sun pierced the windshield, I pressed my foot harder on the gas pedal, fearing to look at the odometer. When I momentarily glanced down, I was driving 90 mph, but I didn't care! I was determined to stay with that Pathfinder.

As this black crusader squeezed back into the right lane of the interstate, I followed. Together, we weaved in and out of gnarled traffic, wedging into spaces that seemed impossible and crossing two and three lanes at a time on the crowded highway.

Seemingly unaware of our mad road race, Christen continued to ask me to pray out loud for her and I did. With my eyes squinting into the blinding sun, focused on nothing but that Pathfinder tire, I continued to speed along behind my unidentified new best friend. For a second, the thought crossed my mind that the driver might think I was after him, but I truly didn't care. All I knew was that he was quickly moving me closer to the hospital that would help Christen.

Every turn of my wheels got us closer. I continued praying out loud as the Pathfinder flew into an opening that did not appear to be nearly large enough for it. I feared following him would result in the sound of screeching tires and crushing metal. I hesitated at the thought that I was going to get us killed, when the Pathfinder driver's window came down and an arm frantically motioned me to follow, so I did. We actually flew across three lanes of traffic and back onto the shoulder, where we again traveled at speeds of 60 to 80 mph.

Not knowing where we were on the interstate or how long we had actually been on the road, I asked Christen for the location of the hospital. She replied it was at Exit 36, as we passed a sign that read Exit 33. Within minutes, the Pathfinder's turn signal came on, and I followed it down the Exit 36 ramp. Christen instructed me to turn left to go toward the hospital. The mysterious Pathfinder turned right.

I followed the sign directing us to the Emergency Room. Christen raised herself up from her reclined position and excitedly said, "Mama, Jesus is here!"

I said: "Of course He is. We've been talking to Him all the way!"

I brought the car to a standstill, and then I jumped out and dashed through the glass doors of the Emergency Room, calling out for someone to help me. Immediately a nurse grabbed a wheelchair and ran to the passenger side of the car. She opened the door and asked Christen if she was able to get out on her own. With the nurse assisting her, Christen rather effortlessly stood up, turned, and sat in the wheelchair. The nurse quickly whisked her away, running through the double glass doors of our divinely appointed destination.

Realizing we had survived our harrowing trip, I breathed a sigh of relief as a man yelled: "Hey, lady, get that car out of here! Who do you think you are?" I had parked in the place reserved for ambulances, so I quickly moved my car.

I called Kevin and told him I had taken Christen to a hospital and that Daddy was in Philadelphia. Kevin said he would leave immediately, but it would be four hours until he could arrive. I told him the hospital was at Exit 36.

I then walked through the double glass doors with no idea where they had taken my Christen. I felt lost, disoriented, and so very alone. Finally, a nurse appeared and immediately ushered me into a very small sterile-feeling room. It was closet-like with a black vinyl bench seat and a metal desk. The only décor was a box of tissues and a phone. She said someone would be in soon and closed the door.

All I could do was pray. I again asked God to help them help my daughter. Christen and I were talking in the car and then she was whisked away. *At least we were in a hospital where someone could treat her.* For the past 48 hours I had been told her symptoms were normal; we would now find out if that was true.

I sat alone in that bare room for 20 minutes. Whenever I heard footsteps, I would open the door and ask any hospital personnel I saw if they would please find out about Christen and get back to me. I asked at least six different people, but no one ever came in to tell me what was happening with my daughter.

Another 40 minutes passed. I opened the door and called out for someone to please give me some information. I didn't even know where I was. I was told a doctor would come soon, so I sat in that tiny sterile room waiting alone and praying.

It was well over an hour before a young physician in a long, white lab coat with his name embroidered on it and a stethoscope hanging around his neck walked in. Holding a black clipboard and pen, he introduced himself. He held out his hand, and I shook it. Without making eye contact, but looking at his clipboard, he began asking me various health-related questions about my daughter as he checked items off a list.

After a dozen or so questions, I impatiently asked how my daughter was doing. He looked me square in the eyes and matter-of-factly said: "Oh, she's dead. Didn't anyone tell you? Yeah, we couldn't save her."

Overcome with a barrage of emotion I had never before experienced, I pointed to the door and told this cold, indifferent, unfeeling human being to leave the room! Angrily, he asked if I was kicking him out of his own Emergency Room. I answered with a resounding "Yes! I do not feel like I can be around anyone that would display such a lack of concern at this moment." The doctor abruptly turned and left. At that moment, the reality and grief hadn't set in, but as my indignation waned, I felt eerily alone.

Within a few minutes, a man who identified himself as a patient advocate came in. He seemed younger than Kevin, and I knew there was nothing he could do to comfort me. He asked if he could call anyone for me. It was then that I fell to my knees in front of that cold, black bench and began praying out loud. I told God I needed Him as I never had before. In my desperate loneliness, I claimed His promise to never leave me or forsake me. I began to cry. The young man, who was just standing there silently, handed me the box of tissues and left.

A nurse then came in to make sure I understood that my daughter was dead. I got up from my knees and sat back on the bench, thinking maybe I had found a person of compassion. I quietly told her, without any tears, that I felt like I was in a dream and none of this was real. She spoke to me in a very stern voice saying: "You need to realize it's true. It's your new reality. Your daughter is dead." As I stared at her I felt nauseated and told her I was going to throw up. She found a nurse to take me to the bathroom, where I stood over the toilet for what seemed like 30 minutes wishing I could throw up, but I couldn't.

As I returned to my tiny, sterile room, my cell phone rang. It was Sam. He had arrived at his event in Philadelphia. Before I could say a word, Sam told me that when he had arrived at the facility he had an overwhelming feeling that he needed to return home, so he told the entire audience that he was sorry, but he felt he needed to leave. Without delay, they had summoned a car, and he was on his way back.

Barely able to form the words, I managed to say, "Sam, Christen is in Heaven."

He responded with "What in this world are you saying?"

Sobbing, I repeated, "She has gone to Heaven."

The silence on the phone was deafening, and then I heard him begin to sob. He managed to say they'd just pulled up to the airport. He said he'd call when he had his flight information, and he hung up.

A woman came into my tiny room and sat down at

the metal desk. She was dressed in a navy blue, out-of-style suit, with no makeup, and she had a reddish tint on her unkempt hair. She introduced herself as the Emergency Room chaplain; she had a small recipe-looking box with her. I sat on the black bench as she pulled a card from her little box and read a prayer about our dearly departed loved ones. I was more offended than comforted. *I needed someone who could talk directly to God, not read a prayer.*

My cell phone rang, and it was Sam telling me that he would be back in Atlanta at 6 p.m. *How would I ever manage until 6 p.m.?*

The chaplain lady took the names of people I wanted to notify, and then she sat at the little metal desk calling them. I listened to her tell my friends and loved ones that Christen was gone, and I began to cry very hard. It seemed so cold, and yet I personally wasn't able to tell them myself. I couldn't share those early moments of grief with anyone until I had shared them with Sam and Kevin.

Knowing it would be hours before I would see either Sam or Kevin, it seemed having the chaplain call was the proper thing to do. I told her I wanted to call Kevin to let him know his sister had gone to Heaven, but she was adamant that I not call him while he was en route from Charlotte, not knowing how he would respond as he was driving alone.

A short time later, a nurse came in and told me that they had informed the surgeon who did my daughter's surgery of her passing. Since he would likely come to this room to see me soon, I was told to stay there.

As I sat alone, another nurse opened the door and asked, "Are you going to come see the body before we send it to the morgue?" I shook my head—no.

That scenario was repeated three times over the next few hours. One nurse asked me if I was going to leave the hospital, as though I was odd to just sit there alone and not even want to see my daughter. I told her that I couldn't go home alone, but my son was on his way to the hospital from Charlotte and I was waiting to tell him about his sister.

Hours later, a nurse cracked open the door and said, "Okay, this is your last chance before we take the body to the morgue." I told her I just couldn't do it alone. She closed the door and left.

During all those hours of sitting in that room, other than the woman making the phone calls, no one asked me if I needed anything at all. From the time they put me in that tiny room, it was five hours before Kevin got there and seven hours before Sam arrived. The surgeon never came. Most of those hours, I was alone with Jesus. My prayers kept echoing; it was just Jesus and me—all alone together!

I recalled precious hymns of the faith that had sustained me over the years. I thanked Him again and again for His promises of truly never, ever leaving us alone. Although those were the darkest, loneliest hours of my life, I knew I wasn't alone. In my deepest sorrow, I felt His comfort.

Kevin walked into the room and I walked into his

arms. I felt a huge sense of relief that I wasn't facing all of this by myself anymore. He was so mature and compassionate, and I was comforted by his take-charge attitude. He had no idea that his hug was the first ounce of compassion I had experienced all day. We sat together in that room for two more hours.

Friends from the ministry met Sam at the airport and brought him to the hospital. Sam, Kevin, and I all three stood in that tiny, sterile room with our arms wrapped around each other, absorbing and sharing our grief. We still trusted in God's goodness, but those were moments of nothing but heartbreak, despair, and darkness. I felt God's grace, although it was veiled by my sorrow and pain. I knew I could trust Him, as He had shown Himself trustworthy so many times before.

As we walked out of that tiny room, I was astounded to see dozens of staff members from the ministry crammed into the larger waiting area of the Emergency Room. They had all been there praying for us for hours and no one had told me. I was so overwhelmed that I couldn't even stop to talk. Just seeing them there truly encouraged my heart, and I knew they understood and cared.

Chapter 14

QUESTIONS AND TRUST

SAM, KEVIN, AND I walked into the house that night to blinking Christmas tree lights and beautifully wrapped presents under the tree; they were meaningless. The only thing that mattered now was my confident trust in God. Even when nothing in my world made sense to my foggy mind, I still trusted in a God I knew did all things well.

The next day we walked into Christen's little house, remembering how proud she had been of it. The idea that she was gone was surreal. Just being there was hard, but we needed to get a few items for her memorial service. As I walked into her room, I noticed her recent journal on her nightstand. Without opening it, I brought it home with me.

Dr. Braund had agreed to speak at her service, and I wanted him to read it before I did. I trusted him to let me know if there was anything in it that I should know. Christen's journals turned out to be a treasure trove for us.

We hurriedly gathered a few of our own things and drove to Charlotte, as we wanted to be in our "home church" the next morning. Seeing our pastor and friends was a balm to our hurting hearts.

I'll never forget my pastor's "chastising yet comforting words" when I first saw him. He asked how I was doing, and my response was that I was "trying to hold on." He then asked me: "What is it that you are trying to hold on to? God's already got this ... there isn't anything YOU need to hold on to! Don't even think of expending another ounce of your time or energy trying to 'hold onto anything'! This is the time for you to crawl into HIS lap and just let Him love on you ... He already has you in the palm of His hand. Trust Him."

His words were the most encouraging and healing words for my grief-stricken mother's heart that could have ever been spoken to me that day, and to this day they continue to provide such peace ... reminding me that God always has everything under control and my part is only to trust Him.

From the church service, we drove straight to the funeral home. As we walked into the funeral home, a flood of memories swept over me: we were entering the same funeral home we had walked into just three short years earlier to help pick out a casket for my dad, the Grandaddy whom Christen had adored. His sudden passing had been very hard for her to accept and deal with. *That day was Sam's and my wedding anniversary, and now we are walking into the same funeral home on Sam's birthday ... to pick out a casket for our precious daughter.*

Christen's memorial service was held just three days before Christmas, and with our permission, Dr. Braund shared some of her journal writings at her service. They were encouraging and challenging to everyone.

My only peace came from God. I clung to His love for me and to His sovereignty. However, that doesn't mean I didn't have questions. The many questions I had plagued me! To begin with, there was a wonderful hospital just 3 miles from our house. *What if I had driven her there that morning—or even the day before? What if I'd been more demanding with the doctor's office? Why didn't God just heal her pain?* The list was endless.

I wouldn't be human if I didn't have questions, but I learned that I have a choice of what to do with all of my questions and insecurities. I can focus on them and mull over all of them continually, or I can bundle them and lay them at the feet of my Lord, because He is sovereign.

I've had to learn to live in His confidence and not my own. I find that even when the worst we could ever fear happens, we must have a confident trust that God does all things well. Even when He seems unresponsive and absent in our pain, wise trust is confidence that all He is doing is good.

Only in trusting Him can I find the empowerment to keep moving forward and not become discouraged. Isaiah 40:29–31 promises: "He gives strength to the weary and increases the power of the weak ... but those who hope in the Lord will renew their strength. They will soar on wings like eagles; they will run and not grow weary; they will walk and not be faint."

My trust in God has been stretched, probed, challenged, and yes, reinforced at every turn. I've found it is something you never master. If we always had strength of our own, we would rely on that strength and never know what God offers. We'd never experience that abundant life. It is a moment-by-moment submitting of my plans, my expectations, and my will to Him Who leads us. If we allow Him, He will lovingly take care of the details in our lives, including those things we don't understand.

I still don't have any answers concerning the black Pathfinder I followed on that fateful day. I believe because I had followed one for so many years, God knew I would follow that one on that day. *If I had not followed the Pathfinder, would she have died at the same time with us sitting in the traffic?*

I cannot explain Sam's overwhelming feeling to return home within an hour of landing in Philadelphia, thus reuniting us hours sooner than originally scheduled. I just know that God is always in the details and I have learned to trust Him to orchestrate the events of my life moment by moment.

He has always been trustworthy and dependable. I could clearly see that He takes us deeper and deeper into a relationship with Him as we trust Him more.

Chapter 15

THE BLESSED FOG

I COULD HARDLY WAIT to get the Christmas decorations down. I packaged them in distinctly labeled boxes, not knowing if I'd ever want to see those particular decorations again. Honestly, I wondered how I'd ever celebrate another Christmas. For our family, Christmas would never be the same.

Although sympathetic with us, Christen's landlord asked that we have her house emptied by December 31 because they had a new tenant moving in on January 1. We were still reeling from the emotional trauma, days of speaking with family and friends, planning a funeral and burial, followed by Christmas Day. The thought of going into her home to pack into boxes what was left of her life left me nauseated. However, the thought of anyone else doing it, only to have to confront those boxes later, seemed worse.

On the morning of December 30, Sam and I headed to her house and began emptying every drawer, cabinet, closet, nook, and cranny as we both cried and sobbed, many times uncontrollably, just holding on to each other as we found yet another picture or memento that stirred up another memory. After hours, we were nowhere near finishing the daunting task facing us.

Realizing there was no way we could possibly complete it alone before midnight, we called a couple of friends who came over to help us. It was late into the night when we finally had almost everything loaded onto the truck to take to a nearby storage unit.

Exhausted, we still had to move her bed. No one had any energy left, but it had to be moved. When Sam and our friend lifted the bed, beneath it we discovered a rectangular box, which I immediately opened. In it I found 25 of Christen's journals going back many years. I closed the box, realizing I had just unearthed what could possibly become an amazing treasure for me in the future. At that point, however, I had no emotional energy to read even one word.

We left Christen's house spotlessly clean, with her house keys laid on the kitchen counter, and we closed the door on yet another chapter. We stepped out into the morning sunrise completely overcome with emotional and physical exhaustion. I climbed into the front seat of Sam's Pathfinder and hugged the treasure box of her journals to my heart. It was another gift from God, presented to me at the exact moment when I was wondering how I could go on.

It was the first day of a new year, and I was living in what I'd heard described as "the blessed fog," a merciful blessing to anyone who has lost someone they love. The agony of grief, like a rushing river filling every crevice of your heart and mind, is overwhelming. Therefore, God blankets you in those early days with a "blessed fog" that softens the depths of pain and loss. It was like a protective shield wrapped around my heart and mind. In those early days, everything you see and touch is haunted with memories, piercing your heart at every turn. While I remember people reaching out to us, bringing meals, and standing with us in prayer, the memories of the first couple of weeks following Christen's death remain a bit fuzzy.

As days and weeks passed, the fog started to lift. I was then faced with the reality that I had a future that would never include Christen. On some days, the sadness was overwhelming. I spent many days and nights wrestling with God. It was hard, and grief is a process that is a little different for everyone.

From the beginning, I knew I had a choice to make: Was I going to trust God, or was I going to sink into the loss? Making the choice was a daily struggle, and I did not always make the right choice. Yet, all through my grief journey, I knew God was faithful in His promise to never leave or forsake me, so I could trust God to walk with me through the pain, or I could try to find a way to drown out its screaming, torturous voice on my own.

We felt the need to return to the Charlotte area. We wanted to be near Kevin and the church family we had there. We began to pray about the move to Charlotte and the financial impact it would have. After all, we had been employed in Atlanta for not quite three years, following the years with very limited income. Sam loved the idea of being closer to Kevin, but he also needed a job that would give him both the time off and financial capability to travel to all of Kevin's races.

Kevin had just obtained full sponsorship for racing in

the ARCA Series and was set to race the entire season. Since Christen's homegoing, we had been returning to Charlotte every weekend to see Kevin and attend our home church.

After just four weeks, Sam received a call from Kevin's sponsor, asking if we would meet him for lunch Sunday after church before we headed back to Atlanta.

We met him, and he began by apologizing for the timing of our talk in light of the loss we had just experienced, but he felt strongly that he should present his proposal to both of us together. He said that they needed to hire a marketing manager and wanted to offer Sam the position. He said he needed both of us to understand that Sam would be required to attend every race. "Of course," he said, "all your expenses for the race travel would be paid, and we're prepared to also pay for your move from Atlanta to Charlotte."

I wanted to give him a resounding "Yes!" but Sam and I had always committed to praying about any big decisions. Sam responded, "Ann and I will pray about this, and I'll get back to you in the next day or two."

We smiled as we calmly left the meeting, but we were both about to jump out of our skins. We discussed the offer on our four-hour drive back to Atlanta. After talking it over with Kevin, praying about it, and sleeping on it, Sam called the next morning and accepted the position. He then went into the ministry office to submit his resignation, and we placed a "For Sale" sign in our front yard.

The next weekend, Sam met a friend in Charlotte who

owned a condominium at the Charlotte Motor Speedway that was used on race weekends. Sam asked him if he would consider renting it to us for a few months. Although surprised that anyone would want to actually live at the racetrack, he agreed.

Upon returning home Sunday night, we found three messages with requests for showings of our Atlanta home. By 9:00 p.m. Monday night, we had sold our house. It wasn't long before we had put everything in storage and were living in a beautifully furnished condominium overlooking "turn one" at the Charlotte Motor Speedway.

Kevin had warned us that the Speedway was used 360 days of the year, but I had no concept of the amount of activity that would be on the track from early morning until evening. The front of the condo had three rows of theater-style seating with floor-to-ceiling glass overlooking the entire mile-and-a-half super speedway.

Our little family was shattered; it would never feel whole again. We each attempted to return our life to normal again, as we dealt with our grief in different ways. Kevin was preparing to start a new season with the new team and sponsor and was also working as an instructor for a racing school at the speedway. Sam had his new job to dive into. They were both energized with new challenges and interacting with people. Conversely, I wasn't even interested in being sociable.

As much as Sam needed people, I needed isolation. My grief was too deep to accept sympathy. I didn't want people to talk about Christen, and at the same time, talk of anything else seemed trivial.

Having lost a child so traumatically, my heart was like a piece of shattered glass that was merely formed into the shape of a heart. I cocooned myself from everyone and everything. I felt as though even the gentlest touch would break what was left of me into a million pieces that could never be put back together again.

I discovered that once again God was in every detail of my life by placing us in this condo overlooking the racing world. I watched racing practice, driving schools, and scores of special events involving hundreds of people. I could be alone in my glass tower and watch the world below. I had time to observe life in an impersonal way without having to interact. It was perfect for me.

On Sundays we went to our church, where I could drink in God's Word. Otherwise, I just needed time alone to heal, time to grieve, and time to contemplate a future without Christen. Sometimes I felt the loss so strongly I thought I might explode. Sometimes I felt nothing at all.

As early as January, we had begun our search for answers to the cause of Christen's death. To our horror and to add to our sorrow, we discovered Christen had died because the surgeon who had removed her perfectly healthy gallbladder had failed to clamp it off correctly. During all those hours when I was calling and begging for help for her, blood had been seeping into her body as a result of the open clamp. By the time she arrived at the hospital, Christen had bled to death.

We began the long process of legal litigation—not for revenge or money, but so that the doctor would be held accountable. For months after moving to Charlotte, we made multiple trips to Atlanta, meeting with our attorneys, who were pursuing any legal avenues and seeing Dr. Braund, as he helped us navigate our grief journey. As a result of Dr. Braund's deep understanding of how each person deals with grief differently, he gave us great insights and tools for helping each other as we were navigating this new road. This also helped us to grow closer rather than being torn apart, which is what happens so often in the loss of a child.

During our time with Dr. Braund, I explained that although I wanted to read Christen's journals, I still was not ready to read any of them. He said for me to simply ask God to show me when the time was right and then trust Him. That's what I did.

Chapter 16

A NEW ARENA OF TRUST

AFTER FOUR MONTHS OF SAM loving his new job and traveling with Kevin and the team to amazing races, this new corporation (his employer) filed for bankruptcy, thus ending Sam's job and Kevin's race team. Once again we were facing unemployment with all of the uncertainties, questions, and confusion that entails. However, this time it was different. I knew we could trust and rely on God to direct us, and we both had a deep sense of peace that we were exactly where God wanted us to be. It wasn't too long before Sam found a new job and Kevin was racing for a new race team.

Sam and I were both so proud of Kevin. He worked hard at whatever he did, but his racing was a source of stress for me during this time. In addition to his racing, Kevin was an instructor for The Petty Race School at the speedway, which had him under my window going over 150 mph for hours several days a week!

On the days when I knew he was instructing, I could see him driving laps around the speedway. Since he was always driving the lead car, I knew which car he was in. Every day, I would hear at least one crash or one of the cars scraping against the racetrack wall. If I knew Kevin was driving on the track, I would immediately run to the glass window to make sure my Kevin was safe and sound.

During one of the times when Sam and I were talking with Dr. Braund, I told him that while the condo had been an incredible healing solace for me, on the days when Kevin was working, I was extremely nervous and anxious because it was so hard for me to hear or see him on the track. I also questioned why God would have put me in a position to have to deal with Kevin racing for a career.

Dr. Braund listened quietly, and then with his usual wisdom, he replied . . . "You are absolutely, totally correct," he said. "The next time you come to see me, you need to bring Kevin with you so that we can tell him that he needs to quit racing. This may be Kevin's dream, but it is simply causing you too much stress!" I was appalled and shocked!

"No!" I said, "We can't do that! He's just lost his sister and is dealing with so much. There is no way we could ever tell him he had to quit his racing career!"

"Oh," Dr. Braund said, "but that's what you were just telling me ..."

"I didn't mean that," I told him, "but I'm still perplexed that God would give me more than I feel like I can tolerate right now."

"Okay then," he continued, "let's try to see it from God's perspective. Do you think there is a possibility that God has placed Kevin under your watchful eye so that you can see what a competent driver he is? To observe that Kevin is logging hundreds of safe laps on the speedway that would be impossible to obtain otherwise without the driving school? Do you not understand the value of the experience and practice that he is getting many days out of each week before every race? Could God possibly be building your own confidence in the career that He has obviously gifted Kevin for?" Dr. Braund gave me something to think about. He again reminded me that God is in the details of our lives.

Over the years, my ability to trust God had grown with each hard situation I had faced and survived. However, during this time of grief, despite Dr. Braund's wise counsel, my hardest times were the weekends when Kevin would be racing. I could not go to a race or even watch one on TV as he flew around a racetrack for hours going 180+ mph with 40 other cars doing the same. At that time, the thought of losing him was more than I thought I could bear, and fear gripped my heart on race weekends, even knowing Sam was there with him.

I would have faced those race weekends alone but for my dear friend Marcia who would drive from Atlanta to be with me on the weekends when Kevin raced. She never once questioned my anxiety or fear, but we would pray through those races. I don't know how I would have survived those weekends without the constant support of my faithful friend. It was one more detail that God took care of for me, until in this area I would be able to stand on my own.

Chapter 17

FINDING CLOSURE

AFTER EIGHT MONTHS OF LIVING in the condo at the speedway, we purchased a home outside of Charlotte. Kevin's racing career was expanding and Sam was involved with every race and enjoying every moment of it all. I threw myself into finding the right pieces of furniture or accessories for every room of my new house, making draperies, painting furniture, and wallpapering rooms. I kept busy but still limited the amount of contact I had with anyone other than Sam and Kevin. I wasn't necessarily happy, but I was content. Sam, on the other hand, was restless in his job.

We continued our legal pursuit, only to discover that almost all of Christen's records had been mysteriously lost or were missing, along with the video of her surgery.

Since her surgery had occurred right before Christmas and the lady who would have filed the insurance had been on vacation, no papers had been filed; thus, there was not even a paper trail with the insurance company. A lab report arrived in the mail stating that Christen's appendix and gallbladder were normal. I also had my phone records of the eight calls I had placed to the doctor's office that day, and the records stating that she had been admitted to the Emergency Room. Otherwise, there was nothing. Therefore, our only option would have been a lawsuit filed against the 24-year-old girl who answered the doctor's phone for practicing medicine without a license.

At our first legal meeting, the doctor's insurance company had offered us an insulting $10,000 for Christen's life, which we refused. Over the next 18 months, we pursued every available avenue and finally one day had to sit down and evaluate all that was happening and discern what God wanted us to do. Understanding that He alone was in control, and that He knew both our heart motives and the outcome that could best bring glory to His name, we decided to tell them we would take a settlement.

We invested the money in various ministries, and then Sam, Kevin, and I took a trip to Guatemala, where we had homes built for several Guatemalan national pastors and their families who otherwise lived in absolute poverty. It turned out to be an incredible blessing to us and for them. Each home has a cornerstone that says "Christen's Homes." That trip helped bring some closure and healing for each of us.

One weekend morning when Sam was with Kevin at a race, I woke up at 3 a.m. and knew the minute I opened my eyes that it was the day to open Christen's journals. I went to the kitchen, put on a pot of coffee, and retrieved the treasured box. I spent hours at my kitchen counter reading and experiencing every emotion imaginable, including many I'd never felt before, but mostly shedding tears over this beautiful, misunderstood daughter of mine. Some of what I read literally tore my heart out, and many were words no mother would choose to read. Dr. Braund had been right about the timing being of God. As hard as some of these words were to read, until that day arrived, I would not have been ready to read them.

Then I discovered Christen's final journal, some of which was quoted at her memorial service. I had placed it with the others and not thought of it again. What joy! What peace! What a blessing that I had these in my possession! Listen to her words.

EXCERPTS FROM CHRISTEN'S JOURNAL PAGES

I have looked into the mirror & seen the face of Judas staring back. ... I have betrayed my Lord!

Wow, I've had a strange couple of days. I have once again turned back down the path only this time it feels so different. I realize what a fool I have been ... to possibly think I could do anything! I have made a new beginning. I had met a God that didn't meet my expectations & now I have turned back to Him ... this time without a "standard" governing me—this time it's only on faith.

I am scared to death, but will not allow fear to keep me in its grasp. I will rise above all of this by surrendering it all. It's strange, most of the decisions I made, I made out of fear of losing control or trying to get it back ... but I'm learning to give it all up & surrender ... then you no longer have the need for control.

I am scared, yet am learning to trust. I think if this was something I could grasp & understand then it wouldn't be faith.

A week later she wrote . . . . . .

At this point in my life, I only have two absolutes. The first being faith and what that truly means. What it means to me is that I must believe above all else and realize I am not in control, only God is. Only through His understanding and with His wisdom can I see.

My job isn't even to see it, but merely to trust, no more, no less. Trust does not require understanding ... truly trusting will not need knowledge but instead action.

The other absolute I have right now is that I am weak & I can do nothing of value on my own, but rather, "I can do all things through Christ who strengthens me."

Five weeks before her surgery:

I feel like right now I'm standing at the top of an Olympic Ski Jump getting ready to go through the gate. Everything is getting ready to really begin and when it does, I feel like things will fly. I have so much at my feet that could happen!! It's GREAT! So ... we shall see what my future holds.

The week before her surgery:

I am scared right now ... tomorrow I go to get my x-rays done & I don't know what is wrong. I am in unbelievable pain ... I am afraid something is very wrong. I must simply trust.

God must reveal himself to me. I cannot do anything to make that happen, so I will wait & pray to have ears to hear & an open heart & eyes to see ... so I may be able to learn & see what He will show me.

I am so happy today ... God allowed me to find my old Bible ... only it feels so strange to me. Looking at these words, it feels as if I'm reading for the first time. I am praying that God will reveal more of who He is to me & help me to find His boundaries.

Her last entry, the day before the surgery:

Well, it is the day before my surgery. I am very scared, yet trusting God. I am keenly aware that I could die if anything goes wrong. My life feels strange. Maybe it is all the medicine, maybe not.

I have this strange foreboding about tomorrow as if nothing will ever be the same after tomorrow. It's scary. I feel like if I do die tomorrow I've been a poor steward most of my time here... there are things I have done well, but so much more I need to learn ...

Her journals are such an amazing gift from God to us. What a blessing that we were able to see, hear, and now read her heart turning back to Jesus! There is no question in my mind that when she said, "Mama, Jesus is here!" that she saw Him as He came to usher her into Heaven.

Chapter 18

A PHYSICIAN'S TOUCH

IT WAS SUMMER WHEN SAM flew to Chicago to attend Kevin's race at the Chicagoland Speedway. During a practice run, Kevin's engine blew up, which meant he would be missing the race. Without a race to attend and a flight that didn't leave until 9 p.m., Sam sat alone in a hotel in Naperville with nothing to do. Looking back, we realize it was the Lord who brought to his mind an acquaintance from over ten years earlier who lived west of Chicago. Some people would have hesitated to reach out to him, having not communicated with the man for ten years, but Sam still had his phone number in his contacts, so he called.

Within a half-hour, Sam was in his rental car, driving to have coffee with the gentleman who just "happened" to be sitting in his office that Saturday with nothing specific to do. As the day wore on, Sam became more and more excited about the vision this man had for ministry. He invited Sam to be a part of it and offered to fly us both there to look further into us joining this international organization.

Sam and his old contact were in communication over the next two weeks, where Sam made it clear that he would need to be free to attend all of Kevin's races. With that stipulation accepted, we were both at total peace that this was the next path our lives should take. Believing we were following God's direction, we once again headed out in blind faith. We put our new home on the market, Sam resigned from his job, and we moved to the suburbs of Chicago.

A beautiful, large, English Tudor, 10-bedroom home to live in was part of the job package; it provided overnight housing for visitors to the ministry campus. The house needed serious redecorating, so at first I stayed busy doing what I enjoyed.

We hosted literally hundreds of believers from all over the world who came to visit the ministry for various reasons. My gifts of serving and entertaining were put to good use. If washing linens can be considered a gift, I honed mine while living there. God, however, had plans for me besides washing linens.

We had been in our new location only for two weeks when Sam came home and said that we were going to a conference in Michigan for physicians and their spouses. My immediate reply was that there was no way I would even consider attending such a thing—he couldn't be serious!

Sam knew it was hard for me to even be civil to anyone in the medical profession. I did not like doctors! I didn't trust them, and I wanted nothing to do with them. Therefore, I was not happy when participation in one of our first ministry retreats involved traveling to northern Michigan to a physician's conference. I told Sam he had to be kidding!

"Sam, God would not expect me to spend a weekend at a physician's conference. Just go without me."

"Ann, we both are expected to be there. Where's your faith?"

"What does faith have to do with it? You know how I feel. I don't want to spend days pretending to be nice to people I don't trust."

"That's not being fair. The doctors at this conference have done nothing to us. Trust God with this, Ann."

"You're not being fair. I do trust God. It's doctors that I don't trust. I can't do it, Sam. I'm not going to go. I know God wouldn't expect me to go to a ministry function and be a phony."

Sam didn't respond. He walked away, and I was then frustrated with both God and Sam. There was no way I was going to spend an entire weekend in the company of doctors. I was not going! It was that simple.

Once again, Sam's negotiating skills—which I usually admired—kicked in, and he persuaded me to go, telling me that the location of the conference was an amazing resort and that I wouldn't have to interact with people but simply be present for mealtimes. Plus, he and I would have a lot of free time together, he said.

I very reluctantly packed my bag, and we headed out for a quiet, rather chilly seven-hour drive. I made sure Sam remembered I did not want to go. I assured him that while I would be nice to everyone, I already did not like any of them. He told me I might like them if I would just get to know them. I told him that I didn't want to get to know them. He said that was fine; he just appreciated me going.

Arriving at the resort, we pulled up to the front steps and parked the car to get out our luggage and check in for the weekend. I was there, but I was not happy about it and I didn't care who knew it.

No one seemed to care what this weekend would do to my mending heart. *A conference of doctors! I still couldn't believe Sam thought God wanted me to be here. How would it have mattered if I had stayed at home?*

As I got out of the car, a nice-looking man came down the steps and asked if he could help with the luggage we were removing from the trunk. I gave him a "whatever" shrug and walked into the lobby of the lodge. Yes, I had to be there, but I didn't have to interact with the staff.

Sam checked us in, and I motioned to the young man with our suitcases to follow me to our rooms. I didn't have any change on me, so I hoped he would get a good tip from the next people to arrive, people who probably wanted to be there. Anyway, I hadn't asked him to carry my suitcase, and I wasn't in the mood for small talk. He put the suitcase down, wished me a nice weekend, and left.

Later, as we were seated for the first evening session, which I begrudgingly agreed to attend, I noticed the forty-something guy who had carried my suitcase sitting near the front of the auditorium. I wondered what interest he would have in listening to a bunch of doctors. I wondered if someone had made him come also but gave him little thought until he stood up and was introduced as Dr. Billy Boring from McKinney, Texas, one of the physicians being considered for a position on the ministry's board of directors.

At first I was confused. Then I was immediately appalled by my previous behavior. Even if he had been the bellboy that I had mistaken him for, I should not have been rude to him. Looking back, I realized that he had just happened to come down the stairs as we pulled up and was merely being gracious when he had offered to help.

I was ashamed of my tactless response to his earlier kindness. As soon as the evening agenda was over, I turned to Sam and told him he needed to come with me to talk to this Dr. Billy Boring. Sam was shocked that I was eager to meet a doctor but happy to accompany me. I introduced myself and apologized for mistaking him for a bellhop.

That night, Dr. Billy and his wife, Michelle, and Sam and I went out for a quick cup of coffee that lasted until 3 a.m. We experienced an instant bond that became a long-term friendship. In the years since that conference, I have thanked God over and over for His provision when I least expected or deserved it. Even though my attitude that Friday night in Michigan was to settle for stale, dry crackers, God still gave me filet mignon. Beginning at the physician's conference, God also gave Sam, Kevin, and me the friendship of a Godly man whose medical expertise would impact our lives in the future.

During the next two years, we had incredible opportunities to minister, and in turn, be ministered to. I didn't have an official position with the ministry, but I soon found myself in the unofficial position of mom-away-from-home to a campus of young girls. My healing mother's heart reached out to these girls and was ministered to by them, as I ministered to them.

The ministry also gave me an opportunity to tell Christen's story, at first to small groups of girls from the comfort of a couch, but within a year I was speaking to crowds of several thousand from a stage. I titled my message "Is He Really Trustworthy?" To my amazement, as I told of the path on which God had taken us, people were impacted. I told about meeting Sam and our fears when Kevin was a baby, about our times of unemployment, and about our hurt and struggles when Christen rebelled. I told them about Christen's seemingly needless death. Then I told them about God's provisions through it all. I set forth the challenge that either God was trustworthy or He wasn't. If we were going to trust Him with our lives, that meant we had to trust Him with every part of our lives.

The more I said it, the more I healed. God was slowly sealing all those fractures in my broken heart. He was again showing me that my future offered more than dry crackers. Even though I would always miss my daughter, God still had a plan for my life that was fulfilling.

The abundant life didn't die with Christen. In fact, Christen was reaching more people in her death than we would have believed possible. People were coming to God as I told Christen's story and shared from her journals. God was using our faithfulness in bigger ways than we could have imagined. I stood on stage after stage and told crowds of people that God was trustworthy in everything because I knew it to be true.

While I was being blessed by this unexpected ministry, Sam was having an incredible one-on-one ministry influencing hundreds of young men, dads, and businessmen. Sam was created for this type of service to God. He was gifted to walk alongside others, encouraging them and stretching them. He loved to challenge men in their faith that they might really know the Lord and not just say they believe. He also was still involved with the racing world, flying to some city most weekends to attend every one of Kevin's races. God was not only healing Sam and me through ministry to others, but He was providing for our future in ways we could not begin to suspect.

Chapter 19

REALLY? NOT AGAIN!

I WAS A JUMBLE OF EMOTIONS as I buckled myself into the seat next to Sam. We were on our way to Dallas, Texas, for a long weekend of fun. At least, that was how Sam had explained it to the ticket agent as we had received our boarding passes. A long weekend was all I anticipated.

Kevin had moved up to racing in the NASCAR Series, and watching the three to four-hour races was the delight of Sam's life. Following Christen's Homegoing, the very idea of racing had filled me with dread as my insides twisted into knots, but I was trying to work up enthusiasm to watch Kevin race at the Texas Motor Speedway for the first time. It was important to Sam and Kevin that I share in their racing world, so this weekend I was going to Dallas. I prayed for Kevin daily, but he was the only child I had now, and the thought of something happening to him could leave me paralyzed with fear.

The weekend did promise more than just a race. We had not seen Dr. Billy and Michelle since the conference in northern Michigan a year-and-a-half earlier, but Sam and Dr. Billy had spoken often on the phone. Sam had made plans for us to spend time together and then attend the race. In fact, the Borings were meeting our plane, and my instant connection to Michelle at the physicians conference was one of the carrots Sam had dangled before me to get me to go to Texas. I hadn't promised to watch the race but had promised to try. The idea of spending time with Michelle this weekend had reduced my level of anxiety.

I knew it wasn't fair to Kevin that I couldn't share his love of racing. I really wanted to. I had in the past. When he was only a teen, I never missed a race where he fearlessly raced go-karts, motocross, and micro-sprint cars and claimed wins as the youngest to do so. Even when he moved up to USAC Sprint Cars, Silver Crown, and late models, it had been scary but fun. In my mind, I knew that the cars and equipment he drove now were actually safer than the cars he had driven previously, but my heart's emotions seemed beyond my ability to control. I trusted God, but I had also learned how fragile life was. Sam and Kevin continued to gently prod me past my fear.

As I closed my eyes and leaned my head back against the headrest, I sensed the Lord quietly asking, "Do you really trust Me, Ann?" I knew I did, but it wasn't easy. I would go to the track this weekend, but I still wasn't sure I could actually watch the race.

Dr. Billy and Michelle met our plane and took us to our hotel, where we quickly unpacked for the weekend. Then we sat at lunch outlining our plans for the next few days. Sam was excited to introduce them to the racing world, having secured credentials for the four of us to watch from the pits with the race team, where all of the action would take place. I was beginning to relax, thinking I might just watch the race this weekend after all, since they would be with me. It was time to embrace the future. As our lunch was served, Dr. Billy asked Sam, "How long have you had that dry cough?"

Sam shrugged. "A couple months," he answered, as he cleared his throat and reached for his glass of iced tea. "It's allergies or a virus or something," Sam told him. "It seems everyone in Chicago has been coughing lately."

After a little more conversation, Dr. Billy suggested that we go by his office and X-ray Sam's chest before we continued our day. Sam responded that the idea was ridiculous, but with continued prompting throughout the meal, to my surprise, Sam agreed. Dr. Billy assured Sam it wouldn't take long. We soon arrived at his office, and Sam's X-rays were completed within a half-hour.

Dr. Billy not only loved medicine, but he also seemed to understand it in a way others didn't. His skill as a diagnostician was triggered by both knowledge and intuition. Michelle was very proud of her husband, and I was beginning to understand why. It wasn't long before a very serious Dr. Billy opened the door to his inner office and asked Michelle and me to come in.

That warning knot tightened in my stomach. If Sam had pneumonia or something else that would put him in the hospital this weekend, he would not be happy. He and Kevin had worked and dreamed about racing in NASCAR; convincing Sam to be somewhere else during even one race would not be easy.

We walked into the office, where an X-ray image hung on the lighted box on the wall. Even without medical training, I could see that a large section of Sam's left lung looked different than the rest of it. This was not good. Sam reached for my hand as I came into the room.

"Sam wanted to wait until you were in the room to hear about what I see on the X-ray," Dr. Billy began. "This large, white area is a mass of some sort. I can't know for sure if it is cancer without further tests, but I do know it is serious. There is a local clinic giving free total-body scans tomorrow.

I'd like to call and see if they will take you. That will give us a better idea of what you're dealing with. The scan will be more conclusive than a chest X-ray."

The room was quiet as I began to cry. Usually I am a very private person, but I could not stop the sobs. *This could not be happening! I had walked the path of loss and grief! Surely God would not put me through that again! What would I do without Sam to lean on? This was supposed to be a long weekend of fun.*

Sam held me as I cried. I knew I should be strong for him, but at the moment all I could do was sob. I wanted to go back to Chicago and make all this go away. I wanted anything but to face another tragedy.

Compassionate and competent, Michelle took over at that moment. "Billy," she said, "Sam and Ann cannot go back to that hotel room alone tonight. We are taking them home with us. You take Sam home, and Ann and I will drive back to the city and get their things. We'll pick up dinner on our way back."

Michelle and I drove the 45 minutes back to the hotel,

mechanically repacked our clothes into our bags, and checked out. I bounced between dazed and hysterical, and she let me express whatever emotion I needed to release.

By the time we reached their home, I had ricocheted between quietly sad and softly crying. Later that night, in the guest room down the hall from these two angels we hardly knew, Sam and I prayed. He reminded me Who was still in control and that we could trust Him with the future. Again I wanted to be strong, but I didn't seem capable of getting past my feelings. I didn't want this to be happening!

First thing the next morning, Sam went for the body scan. We decided that Kevin should not be told anything. At this point we had nothing definitive to tell him, and he needed to have his full concentration on the race.

After the scan, we drove to the speedway. Sam wanted to show them around, and I think he needed to feel something normal again. Sam loved the racing world; it invigorated him. He needed the familiarity and energy of the racetrack and all of the friends and relationships he had there.

I just hoped people would think I was having an allergic reaction to Dallas. My face and eyes were still swollen from crying all night. I did my best to appear as though my life was the same as it had been only two days before. As Sam dragged Dr. Billy around, introducing him to people and explaining how the weekend of a big race worked, I was grateful for the calm, steady presence of Michelle. She was exactly what I needed that weekend, and I thanked God for His provision.

When I saw Kevin, I thought my heart might burst as I was trying to suppress the ocean of tears behind the largest pair of sunglasses I could find. With a quick hug and "I love you," he was off to be strapped into the car. I had to get away from the car before my tears flowed uncontrollably.

As Sam prayed with Kevin and they pushed him to the start line, I was telling God that this time He had really crossed the line with me! All of my life I had heard that God would never give us more than we could bear, and I felt like this was the last straw.

Trying to attend my first race and facing the possibility of Sam having some serious illness, I was missing my Christen more than ever. I really felt like it was more than I could conceivably bear. Once again I was faced with the same questions: Was God trustworthy? Did I really trust Him? What were my other options?

I made myself focus on trusting Him. I understood total surrender to His perfect and sovereign will. I could catch my breath again; however, it was an every-second-of-every-minute effort. If for a minute I thought of my circumstances, I found myself hyperventilating and feeling like I might pass out. I was standing where Kevin could see me, because he was happy that I was watching him race again. I knew the minute he drove onto the track I would go into the nearby building, because I could not actually watch one lap at this point. Once the race started, he would not know I wasn't watching.

I was crying out to God to keep Kevin safe and help

me survive being at the track. I now knew watching him race was out of the question. Suddenly, the strangest thing happened, which according to NASCAR had never happened prior to or since that day: As Kevin was strapped into the car, helmet on and getting ready to go on the track, two NASCAR officials approached his car and told him he had to get out. I watched Kevin remove his helmet, climb out the window, and walk to the NASCAR trailer between the two officials, wondering what had just happened. As the cars began laps around the track, the four of us stood there in complete disbelief that Kevin was not on the track with the rest of the cars.

As a result of a legal matter, the sponsor had decided to withdraw their entry just moments before the start of the race. The equally astounded officials had informed Kevin that he would not be allowed to race. Kevin and Sam were devastated. Although I had not asked God to keep him from racing, I realized I had just experienced another miracle from my loving Heavenly Father.

I have come to understand that although it may give some preachers a great message, God never said that he wouldn't give us more than we could handle. What He says is that He will give us all the grace we need in every situation we face. When we focus on our situations, our abilities, and our own resources, we miss both God's grace and His comfort.

Focusing on God and His resources is when we experience the miracles that give God the glory. He doesn't always rescue us from the storm, but He'll always get in the boat with us! That day at the speedway did bring more than I could handle, but God was right there to carry me through another small victory—I had stepped back onto a racetrack and survived!

The next step was a biopsy. God provided a miracle through Dr. Billy's contacts and negotiations, and a biopsy was scheduled for Monday morning. As Sam was taken through the doors into the surgical unit, I could feel my heart racing, my hands trembling, and tears beginning to flow, as I was suddenly thrust back to the day of Christen's surgery. This was the first time I had been back in a hospital since her death, and the aloneness engulfed me as a sudden, uncontrollable fear overcame me. I was alone in some hospital near Dallas, Texas. I did trust Dr. Billy, but my Sam was about to have a biopsy at the hand of a doctor I did not know.

Kevin had returned to Charlotte; Dr. Billy and Michelle were working. Until they took Sam away, I had not realized how facing this day alone would feel. With tears on my cheeks as I waited, I turned to God for His grace to face my fears. Whatever was ahead for us, I knew God would be with us every step of the way.

Sitting in the pulmonologist's office the next day, we were faced with hearing the devastating news: Sam had small-cell lung cancer, Stage 3-B ... inoperable. Again my world collapsed.

Sam and I clung to each other and sobbed. I dreaded telling Kevin. He and Sam were inseparable. They were each other's best friend. They had pursued hopes and dreams together. *We had already lost our daughter; surely this couldn't be God's plan for our little family's future?*

That evening, in the family room of Dr. Billy's home, he walked us through our next steps, answering all our difficult questions. As I listened to this quiet man I trusted, I realized that God, in His sovereignty, had known 18 months earlier when I thought Dr. Billy was a bellboy that he was exactly who we would need on this very night. God had already bonded our hearts with Dr. Billy and Michelle. I was able to trust his guidance for the next steps in our journey.

Over the next two weeks, we explored every option conceivable, consulting with five oncologists who specialized in lung cancer. Without the possibility of surgery to remove the cancerous tumor, the prognosis from all five was heartbreaking, because the cancer was already spreading into the other lung.

Sam's brother Bret had also begun researching options, and he had learned about the Burzynski Cancer Clinic in Houston, Texas, which offered alternative treatments. We flew to Houston and met with several of the doctors there before returning to Chicago to weigh the pros and cons of our available options. We prayed and sought God's wisdom and direction.

After much prayer and research, we both felt God was leading us in the direction of the alternative treatments. Sam's biggest concern was being able to continue attending Kevin's races as long as possible. He did not want a program that would leave him sick and incapacitated. The traditional doctors all agreed he'd probably need to be placed on oxygen within two months. Although Dr. Billy practices traditional medicine, he and

Michelle totally supported us in our decision to take the alternative path.

We began flying to Houston twice a month for treatments and from there would many times fly to Dallas and spend a few days with Michelle and Dr. Billy, as he continued to monitor Sam's health and bloodwork as we proceeded with the treatments. Their home became our Texas home. Their love and help allowed us all those necessary but expensive trips as we hoped for a miracle. Our friendship grew as we truly became family to each other, sharing every aspect of our lives in our walk with Christ.

I will forever be grateful to Sam's brother, Bret, for finding the Burzynski Clinic for us. Their treatment protocol provided us with a relatively normal existence for 15 months, and then one day we got news we were not expecting.

We silently walked out the door of the clinic in Houston. The same sun shone in the sky. The same God was watching over us. We probably walked past some of the same parked cars that belonged to the talented professionals we had just left. Our previous visits had been so promising. We had rejoiced that the cancer wasn't spreading at all. We had praised God and called family and friends to share our testimony of God's faithfulness.

Today, however, was very different. Two new "spots" (such an innocuous word) were found on Sam's spine. The men we had been counting on to tell us the tumor was shrinking instead showed us how it had grown and spread into two lymph nodes.

Somehow, putting one foot in front of the other, I walked to the car, fastened my seat belt, and stared through the rented windshield. *How could this be happening? How could my healthy-looking husband be worse than before?* It felt like I must be living someone else's life at that moment. It wasn't that my faith was any less. I still knew God was in control and could be trusted, but my emotions were first numb and then overflowing.

We didn't talk much on the drive to the airport. I looked over at Sam, always the rock. His faith rarely wavered, and he was always willing to face the reality of a situation with grace and peace. We returned the rental car and checked in for our flight home. It seemed we should be talking about the enormity of our situation, but what do you say? After 39 years of marriage, we have found that quietness can speak volumes. As we often did, we held hands. Particularly that day, I needed to feel his physical presence.

When we got to the gate, Sam wanted to make a few calls to relay the scan results to some friends. I tried to sit still but couldn't. I needed to walk around. Entering the first shop I came to, I looked at everything and saw nothing. By now, the tears would not stop. I continued to walk around the terminal, my numb mind flitting from one random thought to another as I cried out to God with all my heart. I wanted to appear strong, but my heart was so broken; my emotions were out of control.

I walked back toward Sam as they announced our flight. I longed for the privacy of my seat by a window where I could process this latest twist in our journey with

God. A professional-looking woman approached me as I waited. She said that she had been sitting behind Sam in the gate seating area and had overheard his conversations as he had reported the doctors' findings. She said that she had never been so moved or impressed by a man in the midst of a trauma. Never had she witnessed anyone under such circumstances display such peace, confidence, and faith.

As Sam and I began to share with her about God's faithfulness, another lady sitting behind Sam asked if she could join our conversation; she had also overheard Sam on the phone. What I thought would be "the Gospel in a nutshell" was interrupted by the airline's announcement that there would be a 10- to 15-minute delay in boarding. God wanted us to have a little more time with these two precious souls, as they were now able to share their stories with us.

The first lady to approach us was still struggling over her father's suicide just a few years ago; the second lady was grieving her mother's death from lung cancer. Sam and I quietly and confidently shared God's love and goodness as we reached out to their hurting hearts.

With a twinge of guilt, I was relieved when they announced we could board the plane. It had felt good to share Christ and encourage another, but I desperately wanted to be alone. I hugged my bag, knowing it contained my iPod loaded with Christian praise music. I had two-and-a-half hours of private worship time ahead of me, when God could wrap His arms around my bleeding heart.

Our flight was not at all crowded. As we boarded the Southwest flight without seat assignments, Sam and I commented that we could have a row to ourselves. We were just beginning to settle in when a young woman asked if she could sit beside me. I first looked at Sam and then at the dozens of empty seats up and down the aisle. Somehow I forced a smile and said it would be fine.

I immediately began getting my iPod ready so that the minute we were airborne I could retreat to my anticipated private worship time. My seat-mate and I didn't speak. In fact, my tears were still flowing so much that the flight attendant, showing true sympathy and concern, handed me a dozen tissues. I thanked her with a smile, still amazed that this woman had picked the seat beside me under the circumstances.

The minute the announcement that we could resume using technical devices was made, I placed the tiny earbuds in my ears to search for the first song I longed to hear. I had my praise time planned, beginning with "Great Is Thy Faithfulness" and then moving on to "He's Been Faithful." I could hardly wait. I knew God was as anxious for our time together as I was. He is faithful and always ready to encourage us with just what we need.

The earbuds were in place as I leaned my head back and closed my eyes in anticipation, but nothing happened. I sat up and made sure that the iPod was on and set properly. I checked the battery to verify it was fully charged, and it was. *This couldn't be happening.* My tears and frustration prevailed, but the music did not.

After what seemed like forever, I gave up. Glancing at

Sam, who was reading his Bible before dozing on the flight, I wrapped up the little wires and put it all back in the iPod case and then closed my eyes and leaned back in my seat as the tears continued. I wasn't feeling comforted by God and I wasn't ready for small talk with someone I didn't even know.

After about an hour, a stewardess came by with the drink cart. I decided to sit up and try to read, but before I could retrieve a book from my bag, the woman next to me asked if she could tell me something. Of course I said, "Yes." She said as she was waiting to board the plane, she had overheard a little of our conversation with the other two women about God being in control. She had already determined from my tear-streaked face that something terrible had happened. Having overheard our conversation, she knew she had to sit beside us on the flight.

The following hour-and-a-half passed quickly! My seat-mate had been raised as an Orthodox Jew, and she had met Jesus just seven years ago, but circumstances had caused her faith to waiver over the past couple of years. An engineer from upstate New York on a business trip, her flight had been rerouted due to weather. She was not originally supposed to be on this flight but now believed God had placed her there so Sam and I could help her restore her faith and show her how to let God have control.

God allowed Sam and me to pour truth into her life. She was so open and receptive and had a beautiful testimony about meeting her Messiah and her desire to live for Him. We talked and cried and shared together for almost 90 minutes.

She had to make a flight connection, but after we walked off the plane, we huddled right there in the terminal and Sam prayed for her and the areas of her life where she struggled. She then prayed a beautiful prayer for Sam and kept thanking God for making this appointment for her so obvious and for giving her the courage to sit beside us in the midst of so many empty seats. We all gave each other big hugs and blessings. Then she ran to catch her next flight and we walked to the baggage-claim area.

Sam and I have found that many times, our greatest opportunities for ministry have come out of our greatest pain. The times when we are so empty of ourselves are when God manifests Himself, working in and through us. There is no way to explain how encouraged we were by seeing God place people around us who were hurting just as much as we were. They may not have been dealing with physical cancer but rather were dealing with a cancer of the soul and spirit that eats away at hearts and keeps people from seeing God at work in their lives.

My tears never stopped that day—they didn't stop for a long time. However, we have found God can even use weak vessels as long as our hearts and eyes remain on His face. We were nothing special that day. We were as weak and frail as we had ever been, but we were trying to make conscious choices to allow any and all circumstances that God brings our way to be opportunities to reach others for Christ or encourage the Body of Christ.

We continued to have many flights for treatments over the next months. Although the cancer was slowly spreading throughout Sam's body, he did not seem to have any physical challenges, and as a result, he was able to continue his job and attend all of Kevin's NASCAR races!

Chapter 20

FOCUSED ON HEAVEN

IT WASN'T LONG BEFORE a moving van backed up to our front door. We were leaving the suburbs of Chicago and the ministry that had taken us there. Sam and I had an incredible sense of peace; we both knew it was time for us to get back to the Charlotte area and be near Kevin. Sam was absolutely thrilled to be back in "race country" and began making the rounds, reconnecting with friends and visiting race teams. Although I treasured every moment I was able to spend with Sam, I was thrilled that he was able to attend all of Kevin's races.

Once more, I threw my emotional energy into decorating a new home. Especially on race weekends, when Sam would leave the house, I vigorously immersed myself into unpacking the wall-to-wall boxes. I wanted to make our new house "a home" as quickly as possible.

As I feverishly attacked each box, everything I unpacked seemed to take on a new and different meaning. Overcome at times with feelings of sadness, dread, and apprehension, I wondered if I would even use some of these things again. Each item seemed to trigger a distinct memory. My remorseful feelings had me wishing it were me facing this health issue rather than Sam—he was so much better suited to be here with Kevin now. My feelings of insecurity and helplessness flooded me like a rushing river. It often felt like the pressure was about to break a dam within my chest.

While Sam was still able to do almost everything he had always done, it was becoming more obvious every day that the cancer was taking a toll on Sam's body. His energy level was lower, and he was beginning to lose weight. Kevin was driving in NASCAR for Joe Gibbs Racing at that time, and they graciously invited Sam to fly on the private jet with the race team, putting an electric scooter in the hauler with the race cars for Sam to use at the track. It was a detail only God could have orchestrated. He was the same ol' Sam—with door-to-door transportation for each of Kevin's races! An added blessing was that Dr. Braund started flying to many of the races to simply be with Sam and to spend time with him and Kevin.

Sam and I began reading together each morning from the book titled *50 Days of Heaven* by Randy Alcorn. As we read and discussed the incredible Biblical glimpses the author gave into Heaven, Sam would become so excited. Actually, there were days when I was almost annoyed at his enthusiasm for Heaven. As the days passed, his passion and focus grew in anticipation.

On our last trip to the clinic in Houston, Dr. Burzynski said, "It appears that we have done all that we can do for you at this point, as the cancer has now spread to the brain and throughout your body." Sam had already outlived by an incredible 13 healthy months the prognosis of all the other specialists. By the sixteenth month after his diagnosis the cancer was now ravishing his body, but we were able to continue life as normal with the exception of Sam's lower energy level. He was still attending all Kevin's races and was even working part-time with his brother Bret.

One thing Sam had always wanted was for Dr. Billy and Michelle to visit us in North Carolina, where he could take Dr. Billy around to meet friends and experience NASCAR Country firsthand. Michelle purchased their plane tickets three weeks out, and Sam excitedly began making plans for every moment of their visit. We were thrilled they were coming on a weekend when Kevin was not racing so that the five of us would be able to spend quality time together.

Once their flight arrived, we began checking off Sam's list of things he wanted them to see and experience. Sam's dear friend, Don Meredith, brought an amazing Italian dinner to share with us that night, as he was eager to meet this Dr. Billy and Michelle whom God had so obviously brought into our lives. We all enjoyed a fantastic meal, and at Dr. Billy's suggestion, we "allowed" Sam to forego his special cancer diet and indulge in his favorite meal of spaghetti, which he had not had for a year. We all got a kick out of watching how much Sam enjoyed that meal! We sat around the dinner table laughing and sharing funny stories and a precious level of friendship, finally heading to bed at 11 p.m.

Sam woke me up at 1:00 a.m., saying he had excruciating pain in his leg that he had never experienced before and asked if I would wake Dr. Billy. I went up to our guest room and woke him. Immediately, Dr. Billy and Michelle came into our bedroom and Sam described his pain. Dr. Billy explained that the pain was likely a result of the cancer spreading into the bone marrow. However, it soon became apparent that Sam was on his way to his Heavenly home, so I called Kevin, and he came immediately.

We talked and prayed and told Sam how much we loved him. It was hard and sad and sweet and comforting all at the same time. At 3 a.m., Sam looked me in the eyes and in a barely audible whisper said, "I love you." A moment later, he was in the presence of Jesus.

Although we all knew that his lung cancer was incurable and the prognosis not good, none of us had anticipated Sam's time on earth to be over that weekend. We all had such a great day together.

It felt unexpected, like it couldn't be real. I was amazed that even in my overwhelming grief, I was profoundly aware of all we had to be thankful for. Sam had experienced 16 remarkable months since his diagnosis and had not spent even one day confined to bed. We spent time together every day doing life and enjoying one another. He had not missed any of Kevin's races, and he had been given dozens of opportunities to share his testimony of God's goodness throughout those months. His only real suffering occurred in those last few hours, and God, in His goodness to me, made sure I was not alone. When Sam and I needed him, our doctor was already at the house!

As sure as I believe that Christen saw Jesus when she said, "Jesus is here," I believe that God had Dr. Billy and Michelle purchase their airline tickets three weeks earlier. The Bible tells us in Job 14:5 that man's days are determined. God knew the day my Sam would be going Home.

To say that my life seemed to hit a brick wall without Sam is an understatement. Being married to Sam Conway for 39 years was like a roller coaster ride, and I loved every moment of it. Climbing to the top of each hill or challenge was followed by the exhilaration of sailing down the hill. I would find myself falling—usually screaming—wondering when it would end, praying to make it through and wishing I could stop it, only to be swept up quickly from the bottom to be climbing the next hill! Many times we hit bottom, but we never crashed! Sam would get right back up and charge up another hill. What a ride! Sam's excitement and enthusiasm for every new project, job, ministry opportunity, house, or race was infectious!

Everyone loved having him around, and Sam loved having everyone around us as well. Our homes were always bustling with friends and guests. Suddenly, my world had gone silent overnight. Life as I had known and experienced it would be no more. My only constant was my Heavenly Father. He was all I had during those long, lonely hours, and He proved He was all I needed.

My grief wasn't any more severe, nor my losses more profound, than those others have experienced. I was determined to once again learn as much as I possibly could about how God was at work in my life. I began to realize there was a thread of redemption running through my story, and when I allowed God to control the narrative, He moved me into a future rich with meaning.

Through all of the pain of grief, God constantly proves He is skillful in using broken, hurting people. Knowing that our circumstances cannot make us happy, God enlarges our capacity to know Him and to love Him. I will always bear the imprint of my past. Without the ability to change it or the power to control it, I look to my future with the realization that total surrender to my sovereign Lord is the only credible option for me.

Chapter 21

NAVIGATING UNCHARTED WATERS

I EXPERIENCED SO MANY NEW and different levels of grief after Sam went to Heaven. Learning to live alone wasn't easy for me. We had lived in our new home only four months, so I knew none of my neighbors and they knew nothing of Sam and me. Kevin, for the first time in his life, was racing weekends without his dad, but I still couldn't watch him race. Sam's absence at his races heightened my anxiety, so until I knew each race was over, I was a mess. Kevin was incredible, texting me the second he was off the track in order to calm my nerves and ease my fears.

I had faced profound grief before, but this new grief journey was frightening, because after Christen went to Heaven I still had Sam to comfort and encourage me. Even relying on Jesus, this time I questioned whether I could handle it without Sam. For a while there were people from our church and the racing world who were so kind; however, God blessed me with friends like Dr. Billy and Michelle, our dear friends Don and Sally, and others who remained at my side to consistently love and support me as I processed the reality of another loss.

My and Kevin's personal grief at first was so deep it was difficult for us to comfort each other, although Kevin made sure he was always available if I reached out to him. We had both lost our best friend; my grief of losing a lifelong partner was different from his of losing his daddy, but the loss was great for both of us. More than ever I doubted I could watch Kevin race again, and that truly troubled this mother's heart. It felt like a terrible lack of faith, but the possibility of losing him was just too painful to even consider. He was all that I had left! However, even with my dread, I knew there would be a future time in which I would have to face that fear and overcome it.

The early weeks and even months after Sam was gone were a flurry of busyness immersed in emotions and paperwork details and cleaning out a loved one's lifetime of earthly possessions. Memories flooded over me, and my sense of loss could be overwhelming as I went through items that had once been so important to us but now seemed meaningless. Once in a while I would come across words penned by Sam that God would use to minister to my grieving heart, such as these:

> *I look back and think about what I have learned over three periods in my life. When I lost my reputation, my identity was in the wrong place. It doesn't come from what I do or accomplish. It only comes from a right relationship with the Lord. When I lost my daughter, God showed Himself faithful even in the valley of death. God has shown*
>
> *Himself trustworthy even when we don't under-*

stand. When I lost my health, I learned to take one day at a time and be thankful, and trust Him with each day ... and live each day with no regrets.

Life without Sam wasn't easy. We were invested in every area of each other's lives and enjoyed living our life that way. I had to discover who I was now that it was just me. Everyone had known me as Sam's wife and Kevin's mom, and once as Christen's mom. Those were and still are my most cherished titles.

There is a place in my heart for Christen and Sam that can never be filled on this earth. Yet it was time for me to find my footing along this unfamiliar path of just being me, a process that continues to this day. I came across this quote and knew it to be true: "Grief never ends but it changes. It's a passage, not a place to stay. Grief is not a sign of weakness, nor a lack of faith; it is the price of love."

One word I had always dreaded was the word *widow*, and now I was one. It was hard to know where I fit, as friends seemed unsure about what to do with me. For the first time, I noticed that everywhere I went, things were set up in two's. I'll never forget the first time I was seated at a table for two and was asked if someone would be joining me and the first time I went to dinner with Don and Sally, whom we had gone out with regularly over the years. The three of us sat where it felt like four of us should be. It happened everywhere, easily making me feel like the fifth wheel, longing for my solitude.

A person grieves according to his or her individual personality, but I knew I could not retreat from people as

I had when Christen died. Since I didn't have Sam to walk in the door each evening to share our grief and talk about our day, I had to force myself to get out of the house and interact with others. It was a slow, painful process for me, but it was what I needed. I was facing my grief and my fears.

It was a couple of years before I felt I was ready to attend my first NASCAR race. The race was in Nashville, Tennessee, and Michelle and Dr. Ron Braund accompanied me. With the invaluable support of my friends, I actually survived it. At this time, Dr. Braund was attending most of Kevin's races, and that gave reassurance to me on race weekends and was a meaningful encouragement to Kevin.

A few months later, Dr. Billy and Michelle flew to Charlotte to help me attend my second race. During the race, Kevin became violently ill as a result of food poisoning and had to be pulled out of the car and taken by ambulance to the infield care center. My anxiety was off the charts, but God not only had Dr. Billy there to help attend to Kevin, but he was there for my sake as well, giving me reassurance that no one else could have offered at that time. My confidence increased as I again remembered that God was in the details!

Since that time, I have attended many of Kevin's races, knowing God has been with me at every one of them, but I still sometimes want things my way. I remember one day when an AT&T phone company van passed me as I was driving. I looked at it and said out loud, "Lord, couldn't you have just given me a son that worked somewhere like that with a safe 8 to 5 job?" I felt His Spirit say, "Yes, and if I had, would you be on your knees every single weekend talking to me on his behalf?" After that, I never again questioned God regarding Kevin's racing; he has obviously been doing exactly what God had designed him to do with his life!

Over time, life fell into a routine. I accepted that I was now a single woman with a daughter and husband in Heaven and a son who flies around racetracks at speeds approaching 200 mph. I was creating a new life for myself with new friends and a job. One morning as I was awakened by my two dogs barking, as they did every morning at the first sign of light, I made my way to the kitchen eager for the aroma of brewing coffee. Once my furry friends had been fed, I sat by the window with my hands wrapped around my warm cup and waited for the sun to finish brightening my world.

As I was admiring the maple tree in my front yard, which had turned into an amazing display of orange, yellow, and red, an unexpected and uninvited memory struck my heart like a lightning bolt thundering to my core. It was fall and a fresh wave of grief came out of nowhere as though for the first time. I had marked off several years that Christen and then Sam had been in Heaven, but I was still surprised by the overwhelming grief that always came in the fall of each year.

I so wanted to be like everyone else enjoying this invigorating time when the leaves change and when cool, crisp breezes mark the end of summer heat. For many, the fall season provides that energizing break between the activities of summer and the busyness of the upcoming holidays. For me, fall becomes a weighted avalanche of memories and losses. When the leaves begin to change, I think of my precious Christen and her indescribable pain throughout our last holiday together. It seemed impossible that our last Thanksgiving as a family had been so very long ago. It felt like yesterday and still held both sweet and painful memories. Christen and Kevin had each asked to bring friends home for Thanksgiving dinner, but in an uncharacteristic response, I had said no. I wanted the holiday to be just family, envisioning it to be a special family day with just the four of us, and it had been just that.

Daydreaming of years gone by, I remembered how Christmas had always been my favorite time of year. In my enthusiastic celebration of the Savior's birth, I decorated each room of our house with ornamental trees adorned with lights and garlands everywhere. Our holiday home became a bright and cheerful place where wonderful memories were made. It was all so different now with only me and Kevin. I was still grateful for the birth of Jesus. I could be thankful for all the good times and the beautiful family God had given me, but in November and December I had to work hard to find positive feelings.

The week of Thanksgiving was when Christen's pain had begun. December was the anniversary of her homegoing, and it was also the month of Sam's birthday. On some days during the holiday season, the losses felt unbearable. I had to force myself to put up a Christmas tree, which I decorated alone. Setting out a minimal number of decorations now qualified as decking the halls. This year, however, I had determined to do better, even setting a goal to have it all completed before Thanksgiving.

I finished putting the last ornament on the Christmas tree and sighed. The empty boxes looked as empty as I felt inside. Time had a way of moving forward while emotions could drag you to a screeching stop. Life had not been at all what I had anticipated, but I knew God to be faithful. I had learned to find purpose in my shattered dreams and pain, but the holidays were still the hardest time of the year to bear. I was always relieved when I could take down the calendar and tack up a fresh year on January 1. It meant I had survived another December.

Turning on the gas logs in the fireplace, I curled up with my coffee, my Bible, and my thoughts. If nothing else, I had learned more of God's faithfulness over the last years; He promised in Psalm 68:5 to be a father to the fatherless and a champion of widows, and I had found that to be true. Being alone had taught me more than ever before to trust in God's provision and timing and to seek His comfort at times like this.

The road had not been easy, but God had never left me alone. Through personal experience, God had given me an empathetic heart to understand the pain and loneliness of others. Doors opened for me to tell my story, to challenge and encourage women in so many walks of life. I knew this lonely Christmas season would end, just as the others had.

Smiling, I thought how God had already brought a new opportunity my way. Next spring I would be speaking to women's groups in Mexico, my first international speaking trip. Each opportunity to share reminded me that God would use my losses and Christen's story to help others in ways only God could. Each time I spoke, it renewed my love for God as I would humbly share His love and faithfulness.

Chapter 22

LONG-AWAITED ANSWERS

AFTER SO MANY YEARS, I had accepted what happened to Christen as part of a plan proposed by God, and I no longer needed to ask the question "why?" He had provided in ways I couldn't have imagined. He had answered so many of my questions and reduced my insecurities with hope and peace. I no longer needed to know why my precious daughter had been taken from me, but I still wished I knew what had happened on that fateful day. Christen had been rushed through those double glass doors, and the rest of the story was blank. I trusted the sovereignty of God, so I had peace, but as a mother, I still had questions, questions I knew might never be answered this side of Heaven.

I felt a silent reminder to trust God, so I opened my Bible and began to read His promises as I reflected on His faithfulness and provision over holidays past. Focusing on God and only God, my anxiety lessened with each sip of warm coffee. I felt myself relaxing once again in my relationship with my Father, easing the pain of my earthly losses. As God and I spent time together, I had no idea of the events He had been orchestrating behind the scenes.

After a while, I got up and pulled a pen and sheet of paper from the kitchen drawer to make a shopping list for Thanksgiving week. As I glanced at my phone on the counter, I noticed I had received a text message from someone whose name was not familiar. I opened it and read these words: "Hello. I am attending a Healing Grace Ministry retreat this weekend and saw a video of you. Is it possible to speak to you? My name is Vickie and here is my phone number."

The number was neither a local number nor a number I recognized, and I had never heard of Healing Grace Ministry. *Why would this ministry even be showing my DVD?* I had no desire to call this woman back. This time of year was hard enough without being dragged into someone else's hurts and struggles. As soon as the thought had been formed, though, I felt guilty. I had personally just experienced such a healing time with God, and here He might be asking me to walk along with someone else in their pain, yet I was reluctant to do it. *Come on, God. Really? You want me to minister to someone else at this time of year?*

A few hours later, I received a second message, which read: "Forgive me for being so vague about wanting to connect with you. I did not know how to phrase my request. Last night God touched my life through you. I am a believer and have been struggling with my security in Christ. Watching your video, my heart began to race. I heard your words as the scene played over and over again in my head—a scene my mind has reviewed so many times before. I was the nurse so many years ago that got your daughter from the car to the ER in the wheelchair. There is so much I would like to say to you. Thank you for your story. I am forever changed. And yes ... He is trustworthy!"

Tears streamed down my face as my hands trembled; I couldn't believe what I was reading! I read the message again and again. *Could this really be true?* I had to sit down. *Could this really be that nurse—the one from that fateful day?* I had resolved that there would always be things I didn't know, but now I dared to hope that there might be answers for me. Maybe at last I would know what had happened to my sweet Christen.

I whispered a prayer, asking God if it was really true that He was going to give me answers. Tears flowed as I thanked Him in advance.

For some irrational reason, I thought of all the problems in the world—wars and earthquakes, friends with cancer, people living in poverty and fear. I thought of these and was humbled. God's incredible love for me was awe-inspiring. After all of these years, God cared enough about me to introduce me to the one person who could answer any and all of my questions. *After more than a decade of wondering, would I really be able to learn what had happened after Christen was rolled through those double glass doors?*

I responded to Vickie's message, telling her how overwhelmed I was to hear from her and how eager I was to connect with her. She said that she was at work and would call me that evening. My phone never left my side for the rest of the day. I was floating on air, barely able to sit still for more than a few minutes.

There are no words to describe the emotions that were running through my mind and my heart! I had stood before countless people over the years and told them how totally trustworthy God was ... and I had believed it every time! I understood that the almighty God did not have to give me any of the details of the day Christen went to Heaven. I had long ago laid all of those unanswered questions at His feet in an act of trust and submission. I realized that He was God and I was not. My faith was not contingent on my knowing what happened or why. I was His, and if I never knew until I reached Heaven, well, that was okay.

Now, my incredible, amazing, trustworthy God was bringing the nurse—the *very* nurse—to me who was with Christen when I was not allowed to be! I was going to get my answers! I was humbled and overwhelmed!

Chapter 23

VICKIE

FROM THE MOMENT I SPOKE with Vickie on the phone, I knew we were bonded for life! Through precious tears, sharing, and more tears, our initial conversation lasted over an hour. Vickie said she was worried her call would be painful for me but wanted to answer any questions about the day Christen died. She was unaware of the struggles I had experienced regarding the events of that day.

Over the next few days, we talked several times until I truly could not think of another unanswered question to ask. We both agreed that as soon as Thanksgiving was over we would have to meet in person. My heart was overflowing with a renewed gratefulness and reminder of my amazing Savior!

This is the story as told by Vickie in her own words, the story that demonstrated God's love to me once again as I heard Christen's story through another's eyes ...

"My life was seemingly careening out of control and so I sought out a Christian counselor who suggested I attend a two-day retreat. The counselor began to speak about the trustworthiness of God, stating God was all that anyone would ever need in this life. I was very skeptical. At the retreat, the

counselor introduced a video to demonstrate what total trust and dependence on God looked like in action. The moment the video began, my interest was piqued. The woman on the screen was Ann Conway. There was a strange and strong familiarity about this woman and I found it quite unsettling.

When Ann first mentioned her daughter and stated that her name was Christen, my heart began to race. I thought, 'Oh no, this is why she seems so familiar ... it can't be her ... the woman I have wondered about for all these years ... that woman ... Christen's mother. As Ann's story went back to her son, Kevin, I sighed with relief, assuming that the video's 'take home message' would be about God's provision for the Conway family during their time of crisis when Kevin was a sick baby. Then, the story went back to Christen.

As Ann's story unfolded, I became more and more uncomfortable fighting back tears as my heart continued to race. You see, every nurse has a few cases that become lasting memories that haunt them—a young, 25-year-old girl named Christen was one of mine.

As the video continued, I recalled the day Christen had died. I was the Emergency Room Triage Nurse who had answered Ann Conway's distraught phone call relaying that she was bringing her daughter to the Emergency Department. She said that her daughter recently had surgery, was experiencing difficulties, and the surgeon had refused to see her in his office postoperatively. Ann stated that her daughter was in pain, but it was not the pain that concerned me. It was the description she gave of her daughter's color. Ann said that her daughter's lips were beginning to look blue. She had Christen in the car and was on her way to the hospital. The surgeon was operating there that day and Ann was determined that he see her daughter. Following the phone call, I alerted my Charge Nurse that we may be receiving a critical post-surgical patient. As the video continued to play, the entire scene continued to play over and over in my mind.

I heard details that I had never known, details that shed light on the images that had haunted my mind for years. When Ann ran into the ER screaming that she needed help for her daughter, I grabbed a wheelchair and followed her to her car. That is when I saw Christen. I opened the car door and saw that Ann had reclined the front passenger seat where Christen was sitting. When I looked at Christen, I saw her blue lips and fixed gaze. I knew I had little time to react. If I ran back into the hospital to get a gurney and people to assist lifting her, I knew that she would be dead before I got back and I would have a code situation in the parking lot in front of her mother. I knew that I was not strong enough to lift her and place her in the wheelchair alone. I made what I considered a life-or-death call. During these quick decision moments, I could not take my eyes off of Christen's eyes. I told her that all she had to do was stand up and I would do the rest. Just stand up ... I will do the rest ...

To my absolute surprise, Christen stood up effortlessly. My eyes were locked on hers but she never looked at me. She was fixated on something beyond me. I remember thinking, 'This girl cannot hear or see me and yet she glided to a standing position at my request.' At the time, I was amazed and grateful. When I heard Ann state in the video that Christen had just said minutes before this, 'Mama, Jesus is here,' it all made sense. That is why Christen's eyes had been so captivating. Christen did not see me. She was looking into the face of Jesus. I sobbed and sobbed, realizing that it was Jesus Who had lifted Christen to the standing position.

Once Christen stood, I quickly lowered her to the wheel-chair, grabbed the handles, and ran as fast as I could toward a treatment room. I left her mother behind in the parking lot. I went through the double doors leading into the Emergency Department and ran through the single door to the patient treatment area. As soon as I entered the patient area, Christen was called Home. The trauma team instantly had Christen into a treatment room, where resuscitation measures were implemented but ultimately failed. I knew that what I had just witnessed was Christen's spirit leaving her body. I also knew that someone unseen had been with her.

When Christen was moved to the treatment room, I returned to my duties in the triage room, leaving her in the care of the trauma resuscitation team. When it was confirmed that Christen was unable to be resuscitated, the strangest thing happened. All at once I knew that I was to commit three things to memory. First, this young girl's name is Christen. Second, she is 25 years old. Third, her parents work for Larry Burkett's ministry. And so, these three things, along with the day's events, were etched into my memory along with the image of Christen's eyes. For years, I wondered if Christen's death had destroyed her parent's faith. I wondered about Christen's mother, whom I referred to as 'that woman' whenever the story came up. I thought about 'that woman' so often and wondered what happened to her and again, to her faith.

That night I cried and second-guessed my decision to go back for a gurney. Every time I closed my eyes, I saw Christen's eyes. Guilt weighed heavy on me because I worried that Christen had expended what little oxygen reserve she had left by standing at my request. I wondered if she could have survived if I had just made a different choice. However, in my heart of hearts I fully believed that Christen would have died in front of her mother had I taken a different course of action. In my split second of deciding, I knew that I did not want that to happen. Not only that, but once I was locked onto Christen's eyes, I am not sure I could have made another choice. I also felt guilty because I never spoke to Ann Conway again. In fact, I avoided her. I could not bring myself to face her. I decided to leave that to the ER physician and Charge Nurse.

While the video was still playing, it was as if a light bulb came on ... in that very moment everything began to make sense. I knew that God was trustworthy and was all I would ever need ... shown to me through the faith of one woman: Ann Conway. I heard God speak to my heart: 'Do you understand now? I had you where you were supposed to be all those years ago and I have you where you are supposed to be today. I am the only plan you will ever need.' Oh ... Wow. Truth. Freedom. I asked God why I didn't go to Ann and comfort her that day. His answer: 'You didn't have anything to give her. Now you do.' That was when I knew that I had to find and contact Ann Conway."

As I put my empty decoration boxes back into the attic after that first night Vickie and I talked, my heart no longer felt like those empty boxes. I knew that Thanksgiving and Christmas would truly be different that year! In fact, I stopped to look back through some of the boxes and pulled out a few of Christen's special ornaments that I had not been able to look at for all those years.

While stacking the boxes in the attic, I noticed another box that had not been touched during those same years, labeled "Christen's things." I knew the only medical records I had were the records from the ER. I slowly pulled the dusty box out from beneath the rafter, tore off the tape, and opened the top. There lay a large, sealed envelope with the words "my precious daughter's last day on this earth" printed across the front.

Breaking the seal, I turned it over and pulled out its contents. At the bottom of a page with the hospital logo printed above the words *Emergency Room Records* were Vickie's printed name and signature. I was humbled by God's provision and care for me.

Sometimes I wonder what would have happened if the counselor had not followed the prompting of the Holy Spirit and shown that DVD that day. *What if Vickie had not followed God's prompting and reached out to find me?* There simply are no coincidences with God. He is sovereign and is always working on our behalf, even when we don't realize it. He is always visible in the details.

Right after Thanksgiving I made the trip to Georgia to meet Vickie. I asked my dear friend Marcia to go with me, and Vickie had invited her best friend, her counselor, and her sister to be with her. What a glorious time of fellowship we had—filled with hugs, tears, laughter, and the amazing presence of Jesus. Before we realized it, we had been sharing, praying, and thanking God together for nine hours! We shared our hearts as if we'd all known each other all of our lives … we were truly standing on holy ground!

Six women who had not known each other just hours

earlier were now bonded in Christ—and all because of Christen. Once again God had shown me that He is always in the details. He has provided a loving "family" for me in my precious five "sisters" as we continue to get together, travel and "do life together" to this day!

God used Vickie's story to bring closure to this mother's heart. Vickie was able to answer all of those haunting questions I had given over to my faithful Savior. She has become a close friend, and her contribution to my life is a constant reminder of the trustworthiness of our incredible God!

Chapter 24

IT IS WELL

MY STORY DOESN'T END like almost every how-to book I have read throughout my grief journeys. A knight in shining armor hasn't ridden in on his perfect white horse. I haven't won a lottery or had the ability to travel the world, experiencing glorious sights in a fulfilled life that provides temporary happiness like I'd never before experienced. There are many times I still struggle and find myself digging for cracker crumbs, and I often still feel like the fifth wheel and experience long and lonely nights missing Christen and Sam. Holidays are still hard, and hospitals and doctors continue to be a challenge for me.

Kevin is still racing, and I am there watching as a proud mama whenever possible, sharing in his accomplishments as NASCAR Rookie of the Year, dozens of wins, and a World Championship for Lamborghini. Standing next to him in Victory Lane still brings a lump in my throat, wishing Sam could be there.

Yet, I can unreservedly sing "It Is Well with My Soul" from a place deep in my heart I never would have experienced if my life had been different. I have discovered that nothing is ever wasted in God's economy and there are no "coincidences" when walking with our sovereign God. I am continually discovering the amazing "abundant life" just as Jesus promised and that it has nothing at all to do with material things or Him "fixing our circumstances." It is a place of deep, abiding hope and peace—things that one cannot earn or purchase.

I have found that anything we allow into our heart, mind, and life has an impact on how we grow spiritually and has an effect on the story God is writing in each life. The decisions I make today will determine what story I have to tell tomorrow. At each stage of life, I thought I knew what my future held, and I was wrong every single time. I may have one life-chapter left, or I may have twenty, but either way I want my story to be one of a woman who relinquished control to God so that He alone receives the glory. I can look forward to my future with hopeful anticipation because I am learning to trust in the assurance that God always does all things well and in His time.

Life is sweet at times, but so is the longing for what's to come ... until then, I'll likely eat more crackers and be reminded that filet mignon has already been paid for!

Even though the fig trees have no blossoms,
and there are no grapes on the vines;
even though the olive crop fails,
and the fields lie empty and barren;
even though the flocks die in the fields
and the cattle barns are empty,
yet I will rejoice in the Lord!
I will be joyful in the God of my salvation!

Habakkuk 3:17–18, NLT

It is well with my soul

SUGGESTED READING

STRONG-WILLED CHILD or DREAMER?
Dr. Ron L Braund & Dr. Dana Scott Spears

UNDERSTANDING HOW OTHERS
MISUNDERSTAND YOU
Dr. Ron Braund & Ken Voges

50 DAYS OF HEAVEN
Randy Alcorn

SHATTERED DREAMS
Dr. Larry Crabb

THE PRESSURE'S OFF
Dr. Larry Crabb

A GRIEF DISGUISED
Jerry Sittser

CPSIA information can be obtained
at www.ICGtesting.com
Printed in the USA
BVHW030526021222
653211BV00006B/15